MW01491813

Discussion
do with inⵑ
step back a
plan for huⵑ
fulfills his promises to Abraham, Israel, and David in his blessings
upon Jesus Christ and the people in union with Him—Jew or
Gentile, now and forever. That is what amillennialism teaches.
And when you see the big picture, it is much easier to fit the
individual pieces into place.

—Dr. Joel R. Beeke,
President, Puritan Reformed Theological Seminary,
Grand Rapids, Michigan

In a church culture where the *Left Behind* series is still the
predominant view of eschatology, Jeffrey Johnson has provided
an outstanding introduction to biblical eschatology. *The Five
Points of Amillennialism* is a solid, biblical-theological treatment of
the major themes of eschatology. Personally, I will use this very
readable book as a tool to introduce people to a biblical
eschatology that exalts the resurrected and reigning King, Jesus
Christ.

—Dr. Brian Borgman,
Pastor, Grace Community Church,
Minden, Nevada

One of the reasons believers disagree over eschatology is because
this doctrine involves numerous complex texts and
hermeneutical questions. In this excellent short book, Jeff
Johnson untangles five of the toughest matters to sort out. He
writes with grace and ease, but the reader will note that his clear
prose proceeds from deep thinking about some of Scripture's
toughest passages. We're seeing rising interest in amillennial
theology in our time, and this book will help quench such an
evident thirst for clarity, rigor, and depth of thought.

—Dr. Owen Strachan,
Associate Professor of Christian Theology, Midwestern
Seminary; author, *Reenchanting Humanity: A Theology of Mankind*

Jeffrey Johnson delivers what he promises: a readable introduction on the core of amillennialism without a thousand rabbit trails distracting! His sharp pastoral eye has peered deeply into the soul of our wider Christian community. With a keen theological mind, he has zeroed in on five key principles that clearly guide through the confusing End Times maze in which many are trapped. Familiar illustrations and warm testimonies round out this work, making the reader feel at home. The end-of-book summary deserves a peek before beginning the whole, in keeping with the adage of reading every book from the outside in. For a work of fewer than 130 pages in comfortable sized print and format, Jeffrey Johnson has rung the bell with this fine work!

—Dr. Duncan Rankin,
Adjunct Professor of Systematic Theology,
Reformed Theological Seminary

With the events of our world constantly changing, it seems that more and more people are asking questions about the end times. This is good. As Christians we need to have answers. Sadly, however, at times we do not have the answers we need. Often, we are even confused about this vital subject ourselves. Enter Jeffrey Johnson's new book, entitled, *The Five Points of Amillennialism*. Here we have a simple, succinct, and scriptural presentation which clears away many false notions about the end times and securely anchors a believer to the solid rock of Bible truths. Reading this volume has greatly encouraged me. Now I am excited to recommend it to you.

—Rob Ventura,
Pastor, Grace Community Baptist Church,
Providence, Rhode Island

THE
FIVE POINTS
OF
AMILLENNIALISM

THE
FIVE POINTS
OF
AMILLENNIALISM

JEFFREY D. JOHNSON

FREE GRACE PRESS

The Five Points of Amillennialism

Published by Free Grace Press
1076 Harkrider
Conway, AR 72032
freegracepress.com

Cover design by Scott Schaller

ISBN: 978-1-952599-22-4

Dedicated to my friend

Joel Tiegreen

Contents

Introduction 11

1. The Redemptive-Historical Hermeneutic 13

2. Believers Are the Children of Abraham 31

3. The Church Is the Davidic Kingdom 57

4. The New Earth Is the Promised Land 73

5. The Finality of the Second Coming 107

Introduction

Amillennialism is not hard to understand. You don't need a chart to direct you through a complex maze of proof texts. To understand amillennialism, all you need to know are *five simple points.*

Like the five points of Calvinism, the five points of amillennialism are interconnected. They stand and fall together. What you believe about any one of the five points will heavily influence what you believe about the other four.

Though I have sought to arrange the five points in their logical sequence, they can easily be repositioned to any given order. Determining which point comes first is not as important as understanding that all the points function together. They overlap. They function like a circle with one point naturally leading to the following point and then to the next until it comes back around to the first point.

My goal in this brief introduction is to bring clarity to amillennialism. I have no desire to answer every possible question or refute every objection one may have. This book purposefully does not address the timing and identity of the Antichrist or provide commentary on the seventy weeks of Daniel, Matthew 24, or Romans 11 because amillennialists can differ on these peripheral issues. Nor is this book designed to be a refutation of the other eschatological positions, such as premillennialism and postmillennialism. The objective of this book is not to be a comprehensive resource on eschatology but simply an introduction to amillennialism.

Of course, I will seek to be convincing, but I realize that a more thorough work will likely be needed to persuade those entering this book with reservation. For those interested in learning more about amillennialism, I will point out other good resources along the way, of which there are many. I would love for this book to function as a bridge connecting inquiring Christians to more scholarly works on the subject. To learn about these other resources, pay close attention to the footnotes.

For my purposes, I will be content if I can get the wheels of your mind turning. If I can generate a little more awareness and interest in amillennialism, I will be satisfied. I will have accomplished my objective if this book provides the reader with a basic understanding of amillennialism.

It is my prayer that the King of Kings is glorified and exalted on every page. Even if we cannot agree on every detail of the timing, nature, and makeup of the kingdom of God, may we all agree that Christ, the King of Glory, is worthy to rule and reign forever over all things in heaven and on earth.

1

The Redemptive-Historical Hermeneutic

Two major systems of biblical interpretation reside within conservative evangelicalism: the *grammatical-historical* method and the *redemptive-historical* method. These two approaches have a lot in common. They are both committed to the literal, intended, grammatical, and historical meaning of the text. Both approaches hold to the inspiration and authority of Scripture, and both rightly guard against relativism and subjectivism. Both methods seek to understand what the original authors—whether that be Moses or the apostle Paul—meant by unpacking the grammatical and historical context of the passage. And "context, context, context" is the golden rule to interpretation for both approaches.

The grammatical-historical method seeks to uncover the author's intended meaning by studying the historical and grammatical context of the text. Three elements are vital for this method of interpretation of Scripture: (1) the intended meaning of the authors, (2) the grammar of the original language, and (3) the historical setting in which the author lived.

Redemptive-Historical Hermeneutic

The redemptive-historical approach affirms the three core commitments of the grammatical-historical method. One, we must ovoid reading into the text our own experiences and ideas but rather seek to ascertain the intended meaning of the authors, which should be the objective of all interpreters of Scripture. Two, because words only have meaning if they are understood in their syntonical context, understanding the grammar of the original languages of Scripture is crucial. Three, because the Bible is a historical document, biblical culture and customs become a vital part of our understanding of the meaning of Scripture.

Though both approaches have these three commitments in common, a key difference remains between them—an important distinction that makes all the difference in the world. Though both sides fully agree to original intended, grammatical, and historical meaning, one additional hermeneutical principle guides the redemptive-historical method: eschatology.

Though this may sound puzzling, let me explain what I mean by eschatology. The word *eschatology* is derived from the Greek word *éskhaton*, which means "last" or "end." Eschatology is not merely concerned with end-times events; it is, more importantly, concerned with the end and divine purpose for all historical events. It is not just asking *what* happens at the end of the world but also *why* God created the world in the first place. When the Westminster catechism asks, "What is the chief *end (éskhaton)* of man?" it is asking what the chief purpose or goal of man's life is. To what end or purpose was man made? Likewise, eschatology is not simply asking what happens at the end but *why* did things happen. In other words, what is the end, purpose, and objective behind the historical events of Scripture? What is the final goal of all things?

In trying to ascertain the divine purpose of history, we must remember that the Bible is not arranged like a modern textbook with an index containing a glossary of terms and definitions. God didn't communicate doctrine systematically with each main subject (such as God, man, sin, and salvation) arranged in their logical order. Rather, the Bible is a story—it's God's story. The Bible begins with the historical events of a seven-day creation, then it moves on to include man's fall and finally progresses to reveal the different steps God has taken to reconcile man to Himself. The Bible is an account of God's divine interaction with man. Like any story, it has a beginning and it has an end.

Like other stories, the Bible begins with some key characters (Adam, Eve, Satan, and a male child) and soon establishes a plot line that is developed in its complexity until all the loose ends come together for a single and unifying purpose.

Unlike fiction, the biblical story is historical. It describes real places and real events and real people. The beginning of the story has been recorded in the book of Genesis, and the end of the story has been foretold throughout the books of the Bible. The foundation of the story is found in the first three chapters of Genesis, and the conclusion is found in the last three chapters of the book of Revelation. Between these events is the story of the history of redemption.

Most importantly, there is a grand purpose behind creation and the fall. We learn that nothing happens by mistake. There are no irrelevant characters. There is a purpose for everything and for everyone. We learn that there is a purpose behind the Old Testament stories and prophecies. We learn, more significantly, there is a purpose behind the male child promised to Adam and Eve. We learn that there is a purpose behind the Abrahamic and Mosaic covenants as well as a purpose for Israel. We learn there is a purpose for the life and work of the Messiah. We learn that there is a purpose behind the church. We learn that everything works together for a single purpose.

And for these reasons, the end of the story tells us much about the beginning of the story. If we want to understand the beginning of all things, it is helpful to have an understanding of the end of all things, which makes eschatology a vital part of our hermeneutics.

In other words, eschatology aids our hermeneutics because it helps us understand the conclusion of the story. Understanding the conclusion helps us comprehend the overall purpose of the story—the big picture. And understanding the big picture helps us grasp the individual parts of the story. In any good plot line, the beginning always makes more sense after we finish reading the last chapter. In the same way, reading the New Testament helps us understand the original and intended meaning of the Old Testament.

The Bible was delivered to us not in a single moment but progressively, bit by bit, over a span of forty-seven hundred years. It started with the writings of Moses and would continue to be revealed until the days of Christ and the apostles. The canon was finally closed toward the end of the first century with the book of Revelation.

Understanding the progressive nature of biblical revelation is essential because as new revelation came, it not only developed the story line but brought greater clarity and insight to the earlier parts of the story. For instance, we learn more about the promise that God made to Adam and Eve in Genesis 3:15 concerning the seed of the woman when we read about Christ dying on the cross. Reading about the death of Christ in the Gospels does not change the original meaning of the promise in Genesis; it simply adds clarity to the gospel that was originally promised to the first generation of sinners.

With this in mind, let's consider several reasons why we should use latter revelation to understand the original and intended meaning of earlier revelation—especially using the New Testament to understand the Old Testament:

1. Because all Scripture is inspired by God and has a single Author.

2. Because there is a single story line, or metanarrative, that centers around the gospel of Jesus Christ—known as the story of redemption.

3. Because the story of redemption is progressive.

4. Because of the analogy of the faith, which is the biblical principle of Scripture interpreting Scripture.

5. Because our understanding of the covenants (and their relationship to one another) shapes our understanding of Scripture.

Divine Authorship

If the Bible (as a collection of books that has been written by nearly forty different authors over the span of thousands of years) was not inspired, we should not expect a unified message. If it were merely the product of fallible men working in the murky light of their own cultural and historical contexts, then we would naturally expect the various books to be full of contradictions. To understand the meaning of any non-inspired author, we need to resist filtering what that author said through the lens of the other authors. If there was no divine author, the writings of the apostle Paul, for instance, should only be understood in light of the Pauline corpus.

Moreover, without divine inspiration, how Paul understood Moses should not overly influence our understanding of Moses. Without inspiration, we could not be certain that Paul understood Moses correctly. As it would be naïve to interpret *The Odyssey*, written in ancient Greek, through the writings of Shakespeare, written in Elizabethan English, it would be improper to use the New Testament to understand the Old Testament.

This would be true if the Bible did not have a single Author—God. But the Bible is not like any other collection of books. Each book of the Bible was inspired by God (2 Tim. 3:16). Thus, we should approach the Bible with the conviction that it, from start to finish, is God's word—that all Scripture is without error or contradiction.

We reject the notion that the book of Isaiah must have been written by two distinct authors at two different times because of the supposed impossibility of Isaiah knowing the name and activities of Cyrus, king of Persia, a hundred and fifty years before Cyrus was born (Isa. 44:28–45:1). We have no problem accepting the prophecies and miracles of the Bible because we believe the Bible is the word of God. Thus, because of inspiration, we have no problem understanding the Old Testament prophesies in light of their New Testament explanations and fulfillments.

Because the Bible has a single divine Author, we naturally expect a unified message from start to finish. Because God cannot lie (Titus 1:2), we take it as a given that the Bible cannot contradict itself. This presupposition of divine authorship—which is testified to and affirmed by the Scriptures themselves—shapes the redemptive-historical hermeneutical method.

The Story of Redemption

It is called the *redemptive*-historical method because it utilizes *the story of redemption*, the overarching metanarrative of Scripture, as a lens to understand the various passages of Scripture. Jesus said, "Search the [Old Testament] Scriptures, for . . . [they] testify of Me" (John 5:39 NKJV). The Lord knew that the theme of Scripture was Himself (Luke 24:27). Thus, we should expect that the person of Christ and the gospel message—the theme of the New Testament—would be the theme of the Old Testament.

We see the gospel introduced into the biblical narrative immediately after sin first entered the world. As soon as Adam and Eve brought death and judgment into the world, God brought the good news of the gospel into the world. Though the world had just been plummeted into darkness, the light of the gospel came chasing the darkness. We learn of the gospel as soon as we learn about sin and judgment. At the very beginning of the story, there in Genesis 3, God promised that the seed of the woman would crush the head of the serpent (Gen. 3:15).

It appears that Adam and Eve believed this gospel message, for after hearing the good news of the promised seed, Adam named his wife Eve, which means "the mother of all living." Rather than blaming her, as he previously did, it appears that Adam, by faith, viewed her as the progenitor of the coming Messiah. Eve would be the mother of the child who would bring life and healing to the world. And it was after Eve received her name that God graciously covered Adam and Eve's nakedness and shame with the skins of an innocent sacrificial animal.

This primitive gospel was clear enough to save all those, like Adam and Eve, who had faith in God's promise. It became evident at the very beginning of history that the hope of humanity rested in a promised child. It was apparent that man could not save himself and that there is no forgiveness of sin without the shedding of innocent blood (Heb. 9:22).

From this promised seed in Genesis 3:15, the gospel would be more clearly articulated and expounded as God continued to intervene throughout history. The promise of a seed, the promised male child, was reissued with Eve's descendant Abraham.

God promised Abraham, one hundred years old and without an heir, a child (Gen. 15:4). The heart of this covenant promise, as we learn in the New Testament, was the gospel: "And the Scripture, foreseeing that God would justify the Gentiles by faith, preached the gospel beforehand to Abraham, saying, 'In you shall all the nations be blessed'" (Gal. 3:8). And it is recorded that Abraham, after hearing the gospel, "believed God, and it was accounted to him for righteousness" (Gen. 15:6; Rom. 4:3; Gal. 3:6; James 2:23). Thus, we learn that it was by faith alone in Christ alone that Abraham became a child of God.

The covenant established with Abraham was personally renewed by God with Abraham's child, Isaac, and then a bit later with his grandchild Jacob (Genesis 26; 28). Jacob's name was changed by God to Israel. Though Jacob's twelve sons became the founding fathers of the twelve tribes of Israel, it was his fourth son in particular, Judah, who God chose to be the progenitor of the Messiah (Genesis 49). Eventually the carrier of the promised seed was narrowed down to the line of King David.

The physical descendants of Abraham were special because they were the chosen family that carried the gospel seed throughout the history of the Old Testament. And it was this promise—the coming seed—that prevented God from destroying the unbelieving Israelites throughout the history of the Old Testament (Isa. 1:9).

When we come to the New Testament, we learn that the promised heir of Abraham did not include all Abraham's physical children but only one particular child: Jesus. Jesus is the promised seed of Eve, Abraham, Isaac, Jacob, Judah, and David. Paul said, "Now the promises were made to Abraham and to his offspring. It does not say, 'And to offsprings,' referring to many, but referring to one, 'And to your offspring,' who is Christ" (Gal. 3:16). Christ is that promised offspring—that promised seed. The unbelieving Israelites, who were characterized as having hard hearts and stiff necks, repeatedly killed the prophets that God sent to them. Because of its unbelief and sin, Israel was not the child God had in mind when He promised Abraham an heir. There is only one righteous seed—only one seed that brings blessing to the nations of the world—and that seed is Jesus Christ.

There develops a main character and hero in the biblical narrative, the history of redemption: Jesus Christ, the seed of the woman. We learn that salvation has always been by faith alone in Christ alone. A true child of God comes not by natural birth or by circumcision or by works but by faith. All Scripture points to a single person. All Scripture centers around Christ Jesus.

Because the Bible has a central story line, the redemptive-historical method of hermeneutics seeks to interpret the various passages of Scripture through the lens of the unifying message of the gospel. No matter how much the old covenant emphasized the law and the physical children of Abraham, we know that the Old Testament (especially viewed in light of the New Testament) did not teach salvation by works or through being a physical child of Abraham. The Old Testament makes it evident that most of Abraham's physical children were unbelievers. It is clear that all who were saved in the Old Testament were saved in the same way Abraham was saved—by faith alone.

Therefore, as Michael Horton explained, "When we read the Bible in the light of its plot, things begin to fall into place. Behind every story, piece of wisdom, hymn, exhortation, and prophecy is the unfolding mystery of Christ and his redemptive work."[1] Each passage of Scripture is to be understood in light of its relation to the overall story line of the Bible. This is a vital part of the redemptive-historical method of interpretation.

The Progressive Nature of Revelation

The biblical narrative was revealed progressively. Though the foundation of the story of redemption was laid in the first few chapters of Genesis, the full development of the story went on to be revealed little by little over the next several thousand years.

As we work our way chronologically through each book of the Bible, the plotline thickens, and we learn something more about the story of redemption. As we move through the biblical narrative, we learn more about the serpent and the seed of the woman. We learn more about God's nature and what He requires of man. We see just how far man has fallen in Adam and what hopelessness exists in the world. We learn more and more about the beauty of the gospel until we receive God's final word in the person and life of His Son (Heb. 1:2). It is not until we see Christ in the New Testament that we see the full revelation of God.

For this reason, the Lord said, "Many prophets and righteous people longed to see what you see, and did not see it, and to hear what you hear, and did not hear it"

---

[1] Michael Horton, *The Gospel-Driven Life* (Grand Rapids: Baker, 2009), 94.

(Matt. 13:17). John the Baptist was the greatest of the old covenant prophets not because he was physically stronger or more intelligent than the other prophets. He was the greatest simply because he was the last of them. This made him the greatest because it made him more knowledgeable than all the other old covenant prophets. John the Baptist got to see something none of the other prophets who came before him got to see: the life and ministry of the Messiah.

This firsthand knowledge of Christ far outweighed the knowledge of all the other old covenant prophets. Yet, as Jesus Christ said, the least New Testament saint has an even greater clarity and understanding of the truth than John the Baptist (Luke 7:28). According to Peter, even the Old Testament prophets knew that their prophecies would have greater benefit for New Testament saints: "It was revealed to them that they were serving not themselves but you" (1 Peter 1:12).

Consequently, because of the progressive nature of divine revelation, it is essential for us to seek to understand earlier revelation in the light of later revelation. Most importantly, because the New Testament is God's final word, it is important to understand the Old Testament in light of the New Testament. As Augustine famously stated, "The New Testament is the Old Testament concealed; the Old Testament is the New Testament revealed."

But this does not mean that the New Testament reinterprets the original, grammatical, and historical meaning of the Old Testament. Rather, the New

Testament provides divine insight into the original and intended meaning of the authors of the Old. When the apostle Paul says, for example, that the promised seed of Abraham is Christ, we can know for certain that this was who God had in mind all along when He promised Abraham a seed in Genesis 17. And when the author of Hebrews tells us that Abraham was looking for a heavenly city whose builder and maker was God (Heb. 11:10), we can know for certain that a heavenly city was what God had in mind when He called Abraham out of his own land to wander all of his days as a pilgrim and stranger in this world.[2]

In other words, the New Testament is God's own commentary on the Old Testament. There are approximately 353 direct quotations of the Old Testament in the New, making up about 5 percent of the New Testament. In addition, thousands of Old Testament allusions are in the New Testament, constituting about a third of it. Therefore, the New Testament is not only built on the Old Testament, it explains, interprets, and applies the Old Testament.

Even though the New Testament does not reinterpret the original meaning of the Old Testament, it adds light and clarity. The sacrifices, the temple, the nation of Israel, and other such things are given their fullest and typological meaning in the New Testament.

---

[2] For more on this subject, see G. K. Beale, *Handbook on the New Testament Use of the Old Testament* (Grand Rapids: Baker, 2012).

So, to interpret the Old Testament entirely by historical and grammatical rules independent of the light of the New Testament is to ignore the insight and inspiration of the New Testament authors. For this reason, it would be unwise for us, now that we have access to the New Testament, to seek to fully understand the Old Testament without reading it through the lens of the New Testament.

The Analogy of the Faith

Because all Scripture is inspired by a God who cannot contradict Himself, Scripture is harmonious. And because Scripture is harmonious, Scripture should be interpreted by Scripture. This hermeneutical principle is known as the *analogy of the faith*.

Patrick Fairbairn explained that "one part of Scripture should not be isolated and explained without a proper regard being had to the relation in which it stands to other parts."[3] This is because not all Scripture is equally clear. Therefore, it is imperative that we use the clearer and more direct passages of Scripture to guide us in our understanding of the less clear passages.

For example, because the book of Revelation, with its apocalyptic and symbolic language, is not as easy to understand as the didactic and literal language of Peter's epistles, we need to make sure our understanding of the book of Revelation does not contradict the clearer teaching

---

[3] Patrick Fairbairn, *Hermeneutical Manual* (Philadelphia: Smith, English and Company, 1859), 124.

of 2 Peter 3, which provides us with one of the most explicit explanations of the events surrounding the second coming of Christ. We can be certain that the intended meaning of any difficult passage of Scripture will never be in contradiction to more direct passages of Scripture.

Covenant Theology

Another reason to seek to understand the various passages of Scripture in light of the story of redemption is because the story of redemption has been progressively revealed in Scripture through covenants. A divine covenant is a legal relationship sovereignly established by God with man based on perfect love and righteousness. In other words, a divine covenant set the terms for man being in a relationship with God.

God made man in His own image to be in a covenant relationship with Him. That relationship was established in the garden in perfect righteousness. After man sinned, this relationship came to an end. Mankind died to God in Adam, and in Adam they were expelled from His presence. If God had not pursued humanity as He expelled them from His presence, there would have been no hope for mankind. But God drove humans away while simultaneously chasing after them. He promised the gospel as He promised judgment on the serpent. After mankind broke the first covenant, God promised to make a new covenant with them—a better covenant, not based on works but based on grace and faith. This new covenant would bring forgiveness of sin, righteousness, and reconciliation by the works and death of the seed of the woman. The new covenant would still be based on perfect righteousness, but it would be the righteousness of another—Christ.

Besides the new covenant, which was established by Christ's own blood, there were other divine covenants revealed in the Old Testament: the Noahic covenant, the Abrahamic covenant, the Mosaic covenant, the Levitical covenant, and the Davidic covenant. The nature of these covenants and how they relate to one another is vital to understanding the biblical story line. In fact, the Bible is divided into two parts—the Old Testament/old covenant and the New Testament/new covenant. How do the old and new covenants relate to one another? What are the major differences between the two overarching covenants of redemptive history? How much continuity and discontinuity exists between the two testaments? How someone answers these questions will inevitably shape their understanding of the various texts of Scripture. No one is exempt from this. So, it is important to study the various covenants of the Bible and work through their relationships with one another.[4]

Conclusion

The first point of amillennialism is the redemptive-historical method of hermeneutics. Like the grammatical-

---

[4] For more on this, see my book *The Kingdom of God* (Conway, AR: Free Grace Press, 2017).

historical approach, the redemptive-historical approach seeks to understand the intended meaning of text by the grammatical and historical context of that text. But in addition to that, the redemptive-historical method wants to understand the various texts of Scripture in light of the whole story line of redemption. It wants to understand the beginning of the story in light of the end of the story.

For our purposes, to understand the nature and timing of the kingdom of God, it is vital to understand the eschatological purpose of the kingdom of God. The end helps us understand the beginning. This is evident because the Bible has a single Author and a grand metanarrative (story line) centered on the gospel of Jesus Christ; this story of redemption has been progressively revealed in time, leading to Scripture interpreting Scripture, which shapes our understanding of the biblical covenants and their relationship to one another. In all this, *eschatology* is a vital part of biblical hermeneutics.

2

Believers Are
the Children of Abraham

Whom did God have in mind when He promised Abraham an heir? Was it Ishmael or the Ishmaelites? Was it Isaac? The Israelites? Was it Christ Jesus? Or was it believers?

Ishmael was Abraham's firstborn, so it would make sense that he would be Abraham's heir. Abraham's wife, Sarah, had suggested that Abraham have a child with her handmaiden, Hagar, to secure an heir for Abraham. The plan worked. Abraham, in his old age, had a son with the slave woman, which kept the lineage of Abraham alive. This would keep all of Abraham's wealth from being dispersed among his servants. And from Ishmael came the Ishmaelites, a great and mighty nation (Gen. 21:18).

Abraham's second son was Isaac. He was the child of Sarah, his wife. Isaac would become the father of Jacob as well as the grandfather of the twelve patriarchs of Israel.

Like the Ishmaelites, the Israelites would become a great nation.

Jesus is also a descendant of Abraham. And though Jesus didn't have any physical children, He did—by His life, death, and resurrection—bring life to all Abraham's spiritual children. And though these spiritual children would not belong to any one geopolitical nation or ethnicity, they would make up the citizens of the kingdom of God.

Which of the three—Ishmael, Isaac, or Jesus—did God have in mind when He promised Abraham a seed? Of which of the three can it properly be said, "In your offspring all the nations of the earth shall be blessed" (Gen. 26:4)? Upon whom did God promise to bestow an eternal inheritance?

1. Ishmael and the Ishmaelites

2. Isaac and the Israelites

3. Jesus and believers

Not Ishmael and the Ishmaelites

As we consider the first option, it is clear that Ishmael and his physical descendants, the Ishmaelites, are not the heirs of the promised blessings. It was in an act of unbelief, not faith, that Abraham sought to raise up an heir with his wife's servant, Hagar. The promise God made with Abraham was to be received by faith, not by works. Thus, Ishmael was not the child that God had in mind when He promised Abraham an heir. This is made evident when God told Abraham to listen to his wife, Sarah, and drive Hagar and her child, Ishmael, away into the wilderness: "Cast out this slave woman with her son, for the son of this slave woman shall not be heir with my son Isaac" (Gen. 21:10). Abraham listened to Sarah and drove Ishmael away, for God said it would be through Isaac that Abraham's offspring would be named (v. 12).

Not Isaac and the Israelites

If it wasn't Ishmael and the Ishmaelites, maybe it was Isaac and the Israelites. Did God not say that it would be through Isaac that Abraham's offspring would be named?

The Israelites, at least, seemed to think they were the promised children of the Abrahamic covenant. Not only could they trace their lineage back to their father Abraham, they were given a special identification marker that distinguished them from other ethnic groups in the world: circumcision. Their special place in the world was even more solidified when God chose them, out of all the nations of the world, to receive His law (Exodus 20). For these three external blessings (their law, their circumcision, and their ethnicity), the Jews were confident that they were the people of God.

But such external blessings do not necessarily mean the Jews were the fulfillment of the Abrahamic covenant. Paul made it clear, in his epistle to the Romans, that external possession of the law, outward circumcision, or physical birth into the family of Abraham did not make anyone an heir of Abraham.

Not External Possession of the Law

First, Paul rebuked the Jews for their confidence in the law (Rom. 2:12–24). It is true that out of all the nations of the world, God chose to give His law, the Ten Commandments, to Israel (Exodus 20). Though Israel would break the law immediately after receiving it, and though they continued to be marked by disobedience, they nevertheless boasted in their possession of the law:

> But if you call yourself a Jew and rely on the law and boast in God and know his will and approve what is excellent, because you are instructed from the law; and if you are sure that you yourself are a guide to the blind, a light to those who are in darkness, an instructor of the foolish, a teacher of children, having in the law the embodiment of knowledge and truth—you then who teach others, do you not teach yourself? While you preach against stealing, do you steal? You who say that one must not commit adultery, do you commit adultery? You who abhor idols, do you rob temples? You who boast in the law dishonor God by breaking the law. For, as it is written, "The name of God is blasphemed among the Gentiles because of you." (Rom. 2:17–24)

In other words, though Israel may have been given the law, they were not law keepers. Quite the opposite. From the generation that was brought out of Egypt until the generation destroyed by the Romans in the siege of Jerusalem in AD 70, the Israelites were marked by sin, rebellion, idolatry, and unbelief (Acts 7:1–52).

Though they had the law, they had no obedience. So rather than the law being a reason to boast, it should have been a reason to weep and mourn. The law didn't tell the Jews that they were good but revealed they were dead in their trespasses and sins. The law showed they were under the wrath of God, not in His favor. The law wasn't given to Israel to boost their confidence in self but to undermine it. The law should have led them to repentance, not self-confidence.

The law said, "Do and live." But it also said, "Cursed is the one who does not do everything that is written in the law" (Deut. 27:26). Ezekiel warned Israel that God would kill them if they did not abide in obedience: "Though I say to the righteous that he shall surely live, yet if he trusts in his righteousness and does injustice, none of his righteous deeds shall be remembered, but in his injustice that he has done he shall die" (Ezek. 33:13).

Because God knew the law could not bring obedience to those enslaved to sin, He didn't give the law to the Jews for them to try to gain a works righteousness (Rom. 3:20). God knew this was an impossibility. Instead, God gave the law to Israel to take away their boasting and to bring them to their knees (Rom. 3:19). As with the gentiles, the Jews were born enslaved to sin. They were sinners. Paul made it clear that "none is righteous, no, not one" (v. 10). Giving Israel the law, written in stone, was not going to change their hearts of stone.

Rather, the law was given to Israel to be a schoolmaster. It was to be a teacher that pointed them away from themselves to see their need for the promised child—Christ Jesus (Gal. 3:24).

Israel was so prideful that they misused the law. They took the very thing designed to humble them and turned it into a means of self-righteousness and pride. The Jews used the very thing that told them they were no better than the gentiles to make themselves feel superior to the gentiles. "Unlike the lawless gentiles, we have the law," so they thought to themselves.

Not only did Paul rebuke the Jews for their misuse of the law but he rebuked them for their pride in thinking they were the only ones who possessed the law. According to the Jews, the gentiles were lawless because they were without law. The gentiles didn't know any better. On the other hand, because the Jews were children of the Mosaic covenant, they were not like the ignorant gentiles. They at least knew the difference between right and wrong.

Such pride, however, was also baseless. The Jews had no reason to feel special. Even the gentiles know the difference between right and wrong, for Paul said, God has written His law on their conscience (Rom. 2:14–15). So, according to Paul, Israel had no reason to think they were any better than the heathen nations. Both were sinful.

Both had come short of the glory of God. Both were under the wrath of God. And both had been instructed in the law of God. Such boasting, therefore, was unfounded.

Not Outward Circumcision

The second blessing that Abraham's physical children boasted in was their circumcision. There was nothing that identified a Jew's Jewishness more than circumcision—the sign or badge of being a child of Abraham. For the Jews, circumcision was vital. It marked them as God's covenant people. It separated and distinguished them from every other nation and people group in the world. It was so important to the Jews that those who refused to be circumcised were cut off from the covenant community (Gen. 17:14). Yet this, too, according to Paul, had no lasting significance in identifying who God's true people are: "For circumcision indeed is of value if you obey the law, but if you break the law, your circumcision becomes uncircumcision" (Rom. 2:25).

This is not just a New Testament reinterpretation of the significance of circumcision. No, the Old Testament makes it clear that circumcision didn't transform a physical child of Abraham into a spiritual child of Abraham. According to Moses, more than physical circumcision was needed for a physical child of Abraham to become a member of God's people. In fact, Moses commanded the Israelites to circumcise their hearts (Deut. 10:16). Spiritual circumcision, which is a circumcision of the heart, is what is needed for someone to be right with God.

Moses knew that such a command was impossible to fulfill. The inward circumcision of the heart is something only the Holy Spirit can apply (Deut. 30:6). It is impossible for those born of flesh and for those who live in the flesh to please God (Rom. 8:8). Just as it is impossible to be the cause of your own natural birth, it is impossible to circumcise your own heart and be the cause of your own spiritual birth.

Because those born of the flesh, even those born of Abraham's flesh, cannot please God, they, being members of Adam's fallen race, are born under the wrath of God (Eph. 2:3). And until the Jews could circumcise their hearts, they would have no hope of escaping God's wrath either (Jer. 4:4). Thus, Jeremiah warned of the judgment that was certain to come upon Israel: "'Behold, the days are coming, declares the Lord, when I will punish all those who are circumcised . . . in the flesh . . . [yet] uncircumcised in heart" (Jer. 9:25–26).

So, what value does physical circumcision have for the Jews? If physical circumcision didn't secure participation in Abraham's inheritance, what merit did it have? Like the law, circumcision would have been of great value if it would have been used correctly. Rather than circumcision being a means of self-confidence, it should have been used as a reason to reject all confidence in the flesh. What Israel needed, as evidenced by physical circumcision, was inward circumcision of the heart—a circumcision they could not perform. They should have known by their physical circumcision that they could not please God in their flesh. Circumcision should have displayed their need for the Spirit and the Messiah.

To take confidence in physical circumcision, according to Paul, was the same thing as taking confidence in the law. Because the Jews should have known that they couldn't keep the law, they also should have known not to boast in their circumcision. Paul said, "For circumcision indeed is of value if you obey the law, but if you break the law, your circumcision becomes uncircumcision" (Rom. 2:25). According to Paul, the Jews couldn't properly claim to be a true Jew—a real child of Abraham—just because they were circumcised in the flesh: "For no one is a Jew who is merely one outwardly, nor is circumcision outward and physical" (v. 28).

Who is a Jew then? Who is the true heir of Abraham? Paul went on to answer: "But a Jew is one inwardly, and circumcision is a matter of the heart, by the Spirit, not by the letter. His praise is not from man but from God" (v. 29). This is why Paul tells believers, both Jews and gentiles:

In him also you were circumcised with a circumcision made without hands, by putting off the body of the flesh, by the circumcision of Christ, having been buried with him in baptism, in which you were also raised with him through faith in the powerful working of God, who raised him from the dead. And you, who were dead in your trespasses and the uncircumcision of your flesh, God made alive together with him, having forgiven us all our trespasses, by canceling the record of debt that stood against us with its legal demands. This he set aside, nailing it to the cross. He disarmed the rulers and authorities and put them to open shame, by triumphing over them in him. (Col. 2:11–15)

This is the inward circumcision that Moses talked about. This is the circumcision of the heart that can come only by spiritual regeneration. This is the inward circumcision that comes only by God's grace and takes away any confidence in the flesh: "For we are the circumcision, who worship by the Spirit of God and glory in Christ Jesus and put no confidence in the flesh" (Phil. 3:3).

Because it is faith alone that makes someone a child of Abraham, there remains no room for boasting. The Jews' boasting also opens the door for the uncircumcised gentiles to enter into the covenant blessings of Abraham:

Then what becomes of our boasting? It is excluded. By what kind of law? By a law of works? No, but by the law of faith. For we hold that one is justified by faith apart from works of the law. Or is God the God of Jews only? Is he not the God of Gentiles also? Yes, of Gentiles also, since God is one—who will justify the circumcised by faith and the uncircumcised through faith. (Rom. 3:27–31)

And anyone who would argue that Abraham's circumcision was a sign and seal of an imputed righteousness that comes by faith must keep in mind that Abraham had faith and was justified before (not after) he was circumcised. The chronological order of Abraham's faith and circumcision is a crucial detail for the apostle Paul, for this order indicates that Abraham is the father of all who believe (both Jews and gentiles) and are justified even without circumcision:

> Is this blessing then only for the circumcised, or also for the uncircumcised? For we say that faith was counted to Abraham as righteousness. How then was it counted to him? Was it before or after he had been circumcised? It was not after, but before he was circumcised. He received the sign of circumcision as a seal of the righteousness that he had by faith while he was still uncircumcised. The purpose was to make him the father of all who believe without being circumcised, so that righteousness would be counted to them as well, and to make him the father of the circumcised who are not merely circumcised but who also walk in the footsteps of the faith that our father Abraham had before he was circumcised. (Rom. 4:9–12)

Thus, Abraham being justified by faith, without circumcision, shows how he can be the father of all those who are justified by faith (with or without circumcision).

Not Physical Birth

Some may object by saying circumcision doesn't make a gentile a true Jew any more than water baptism makes a sinner a true born-again Christian. A true Jew is one who is born a Jew. A true child of Abraham is not a gentile proselyte that identifies with the Jewish people through circumcision but a natural born child who can trace his or her biological lineage back to Abraham. This is the real Jew.

Not only was this not the case for Esau, apparently it wasn't the case for most of Abraham's physical children. Though many Jews can trace their family lineage back to Abraham, they were cut off from the inheritance of Abraham because of unbelief while many gentiles have been grafted into his heritance because of faith. Jesus said, "Truly, I tell you, with no one in Israel have I found such faith. I tell you, many will come from east and west and recline at table with Abraham, Isaac, and Jacob in the kingdom of heaven, while the sons of the kingdom will be thrown into the outer darkness. In that place there will be weeping and gnashing of teeth" (Matt. 8:10–12).

Knowing this, the Lord warned the Jews not to trust in family lineage. Just because the Jews could trace their heritage back to their father Abraham didn't mean they were the heirs of Abraham. "And do not presume to say to yourselves," the Lord said, "'We have Abraham as our father,' for I tell you, God is able from these stones to raise up children for Abraham" (Matt. 3:9).

For the self-righteous Jews, such teaching was hard to receive. Most of the Jews even hated Christ because of it. Their rich heritage, their possession of the law, their circumcision, and even their family lineage was too much for many of them to reject. It is hard enough to turn from one's sins, but even harder to turn from one's perceived righteousness. For the Jews to reject their own Jewishness, the very thing they trusted in, and to view it as rubbish, as the apostle Paul did (Phil. 3:8), was impossible. Yet a total rejection of self is the terms of the gospel.

The Jews had an even harder time accepting that the uncircumcised gentiles could enter into the promised inheritance without any merit or worthiness. It was difficult for the Jews to conceive that dirty dogs could receive the inheritance of Abraham—and even harder to conceive that these dirty dogs didn't have to submit to circumcision. For the unworthy prodigal son, according to the older son, to get the party and fatted calf is simply not fair (Luke 15:11–32).

For a physical Jew to become a spiritual Jew, he or she had to reject their birthright and plead for mercy in faith. Unworthy gentiles don't have to become like the self-righteous Jews; the self-righteous Jews have to become like the unworthy gentiles. It was the unworthy and repentant tax collector who left the temple justified, according to Christ, and not the self-righteous Pharisee (Luke 18:9–14). The only way to become a child of Abraham, according to Paul, was to become like the dirty gentiles—to become a sinner in need of forgiveness:

> For the promise to Abraham and his offspring that he would be heir of the world did not come through the

law but through the righteousness of faith. For if it is the adherents of the law who are to be the heirs, faith is null and the promise is void. For the law brings wrath, but where there is no law there is no transgression.

That is why it depends on faith, in order that the promise may rest on grace and be guaranteed to all his offspring—not only to the adherent of the law but also to the one who shares the faith of Abraham, who is the father of us all, as it is written, "I have made you the father of many nations"—in the presence of the God in whom he believed, who gives life to the dead and calls into existence the things that do not exist. In hope he believed against hope, that he should become the father of many nations, as he had been told, "So shall your offspring be." (Rom. 4:13–18)

In short, in the same way physical circumcision does not secure spiritual circumcision, being born a physical Jew did not make someone a spiritual Jew. The true children of Abraham are those, and only those, who have the same faith as Abraham. The true children of Abraham are those who are born of the Spirit and not of the flesh. The true children of Abraham are those who not only have the faith of Abraham but the good works of Abraham: "They answered him, 'Abraham is our father.' Jesus said to them, 'If you were Abraham's children, you would be doing the works Abraham did, but now you seek to kill me, a man who has told you the truth that I heard from God. This is not what Abraham did'" (John 8:39–40).

Does faith alone not leave out the majority of Israel? Throughout their history, Israel has been marked by unbelief and disobedience. Does their unbelief make God unfaithful in His promise to Abraham? Is God obligated to bless the nation of Israel because of His covenant promise to the children of Israel? Paul answers no: "But it is not as though the word of God has failed. For not all who are descended from Israel belong to Israel, and not all are children of Abraham because they are his offspring, but 'Through Isaac shall your offspring be named.' This means that it is not the children of the flesh who are the children of God, but the children of the promise are counted as offspring" (Rom. 9:6–8).

In other words, Esau is evidence that God's promise to Abraham does not obligate Him to save every physical child of Abraham. Esau had all the qualifications to be an heir of Abraham, even more so than his younger brother, Jacob. But, no, the inheritance didn't go to Esau any more than it went to Ishmael. Esau, though he was a circumcised child of Abraham, was not the heir of Abraham. And this should have been a warning to all the Jews.

Consequently, according to Paul, "Not all who are descended from Israel belong to Israel, and not all are children of Abraham because they are his offspring" (Rom. 9:6–7). But the fact that "not all Israel is of Israel" does not mean that God is unfaithful to His promise to Abraham. This is because the children of promise were not selected by physical birthright but by divine election.

So, just as the Ishmaelites were not the intended fulfillment of the Abrahamic covenant, the unbelieving Israelites were not the true children of God.

Christ Is the Seed of Abraham

If the unbelieving Jews (and this was most of them) weren't the promised children of Abraham, then who are the real children of Abraham? More importantly, how is it possible for non-Jewish people to become the rightful heirs of Abraham?

The answer is found *not* in a New Testament reinterpretation or spiritualization of the Abrahamic covenant but in the original wording of the Abrahamic covenant. Paul goes back to Genesis 17 and examines the fine print. He wants to interpret every word of the covenant precisely and literally. And what Paul points out about the Abrahamic covenant is that God only had one particular child in mind when God promised Abraham a seed: "Now the promises were made to Abraham and to his offspring. It does not say, 'And to offsprings,' referring to many, but referring to one" (Gal. 3:16).

What does it mean that God only had one particular child in mind when He promised Abraham an heir? And more significantly, who is that one seed of Abraham? Clearly, it was not Ishmael or Esau. But it must have not been Isaac or Jacob either. In fact, it couldn't have been Isaac or Jacob because God promised both Isaac (Gen. 26:1–5) and Jacob (Gen. 35:9–15) that they would be the *father* of the promised seed. If either of them would have been the chosen seed, then God wouldn't have promised that they, like Abraham, would be the father, the progenitor, of *the* promised seed. In other words, you can't be the promised child if you are the father of the promised child.

So, if the promised child was not Ishmael, Isaac, Esau, or Jacob, then who was it? Who was the promised child that God had in mind when He promised Abraham, Isaac, and Jacob a son? According to Paul, the fulfillment of the Abrahamic covenant is Jesus Christ: "'And to offsprings,' referring to many, but referring to one, 'And to your offspring,' who is Christ" (Gal. 3:16).

And as Isaac was the sole heir of Abraham's physical possessions, Jesus is the sole heir of Abraham's spiritual possessions. This is important to note. Isaac didn't receive any of the inheritance that God promised to give to the seed of Abraham. This is because Abraham didn't have it to pass down to Isaac. For it is reported that Abraham wandered in a strange land without receiving any of the promised inheritance and "died in faith, not having received the things promised, but having seen them and greeted them from afar, and having acknowledged that [he was a stranger] and [exile] on the earth" (Heb. 11:13).

Abraham knew the promised inheritance was something far greater than temporary wealth, "for he was looking forward to the city that has foundations, whose designer and builder is God" (Heb. 11:10). Abraham knew that the inheritance was something eternal. And because this heavenly and eternal inheritance was not yet received by Abraham, he didn't have it to pass down to Isaac. All Abraham had to give to Isaac were the temporal possessions accumulated throughout his life—possessions that have long since passed away. It is certain there was nothing of Abraham's personal belongings left for Jesus to inherit.

Moreover, Israel, after coming out of Egypt, may have taken over the land of Canaan, but this, too, was not the heavenly city God had in mind, because the heavenly city was promised to a single child of Abraham—Jesus Christ.

Though Abraham's physical belonging were passed on and divided among his physical children, only the Lord Jesus, the promised seed of Abraham, has been given the full spiritual inheritance of Abraham. As *the* seed of Abraham, Christ has been "appointed [to be] the heir of all things" (Heb. 1:2). From the nations of the world to the ends of the earth, all has been given to Christ as an eternal possession (Ps. 2:8).

But how does Christ's being the sole inheritor bring blessings to the nations of the world? Was not the promise of the Abrahamic covenant to bring blessings to all the nations of the world?

Though Christ didn't have any biological children, He did secure righteousness, life, and resurrection for all those who believe in Him. He brought spiritual and eternal life to those God had given to Him even while they were dead in their trespasses and sins. The life Christ provides is supernatural—it is a life that brings a rebirth more miraculous than the birth of Isaac. Though Isaac was born when Sarah was old and barren, believers are reborn when they are dead in their sins. The birth of Isaac may have been miraculous, but it was still a natural birth. The birth of believers is altogether supernatural. Though death is certain to overtake all Abraham's physical children, all his spiritual children "shall never die" (John 11:26).

By faith alone, believers are united to the very righteousness, resurrection, and life of Christ. Christ's life becomes their life. The heavenly and eternal city promised to Abraham has been secured by the child of Abraham (John 14:3). And by His life, death, and resurrection, Christ brings "many sons to glory" (Heb. 2:10).

The interesting thing is that Christ does not take His inheritance and piece it out until He becomes depleted. Now that Christ has risen from the dead, He cannot die a second time. Thus, He doesn't leave His inheritance to any successor. Moreover, Christ does not cease to own everything as He bestows everything He has on His followers.

But how can Christ keep that which He gives away? And how can each believer receive not a portion but the full inheritance? How can each believer equally receive everything that belongs to Christ?

The answer to these difficult questions is found in the nature of salvation and how faith unites believers to Christ.

When believers are united to Christ by faith, they are united to all that is in Christ. Believers receive not just a part of the life and righteousness of Christ; they receive the full life and righteousness of Christ. By being united to Christ, believers become joint heirs with Christ. All that belongs to Christ belongs to those in Christ (1 Cor. 3:21). In this way Christ keeps all that He gives to His followers.

And if Christ is the sole heir of Abraham, then all those united to Christ by faith, both believing Jews and believing gentiles, are united to the full inheritance of Abraham. "And if you are Christ's, then you are Abraham's offspring, heirs according to promise" (Gal. 3:29). As Sam Storms writes, "Since the Church is the body of Christ, of which he himself is the Head, what God intended for him, God also intended for her. What is true of him is true of her. *Both Jesus and his body, the Church, constitute the true Israel in and for whom all the promises of the Old Testament find their fulfillment.*"[5]

For this reason, within Christ, there is no difference between Jew and gentile (Gal. 3:28). The inheritance promised to Abraham is received by the heirs of Abraham in the same way it was received by Abraham himself. Even Abraham became an heir of the promise not by ethnicity, works of the law, or circumcision:

---

[5] Sam Storms, *Kingdom Come: The Amillennial Alternative* (Ross-shire, UK: Mentor, 2013), 42.

Is this blessing then only for the circumcised, or also for the uncircumcised? For we say that faith was counted to Abraham as righteousness. How then was it counted to him? Was it before or after he had been circumcised? It was not after, but before he was circumcised. He received the sign of circumcision as a seal of the righteousness that he had by faith while he was still uncircumcised. The purpose was to make him the father of all who believe without being circumcised, so that righteousness would be counted to them as well, and to make him the father of the circumcised who are not merely circumcised but who also walk in the footsteps of the faith that our father Abraham had before he was circumcised. (Rom. 4:9–12)

Thus, the inheritance is not by law, circumcision, genetics, or birthright but by promise, and the promise can be received by faith alone by both Jews and gentiles:

This is what I mean: the law, which came 430 years afterward, does not annul a covenant previously ratified by God, so as to make the promise void. For if the inheritance comes by the law, it no longer comes by promise; but God gave it to Abraham by a promise. (Gal. 3:17–18)

And in this way, both believing Jews and gentiles (without the law, circumcision, and genetics) become the heirs and children of Abraham:

Know then that it is those of faith who are the sons of Abraham. And the Scripture, foreseeing that God would justify the Gentiles by faith, preached the gospel beforehand to Abraham, saying, "In you shall all the nations be blessed." So then, those who are of faith are blessed along with Abraham, the man of faith. (Gal. 3:7–9)

The Church Does Not Replace Israel

Paul wanted to make it clear that believers were not taking the place of Israel. This is not a bait-and-switch theology. It is not as if the New Testament finds a novel way of understanding the original meaning of the Abrahamic covenant. Rather, to explain the original meaning of the Abrahamic covenant, Paul compares physical Israel with Ishmael and believers with Isaac:

> For it is written that Abraham had two sons, one by a slave woman and one by a free woman. But the son of the slave was born according to the flesh, while the son of the free woman was born through promise. Now this may be interpreted allegorically: these women are two covenants. One is from Mount Sinai, bearing children for slavery; she is Hagar. Now Hagar is Mount Sinai in Arabia; she corresponds to the present Jerusalem, for she is in slavery with her children. But the Jerusalem above is free, and she is our mother. For it is written,

> "Rejoice, O barren one who does not bear;
>   break forth and cry aloud, you who are not in labor!
> For the children of the desolate one will be more
>   than those of the one who has a husband."

Now you, brothers, like Isaac, are children of promise. But just as at that time he who was born according to the flesh persecuted him who was born according to the Spirit, so also it is now. But what does the Scripture say? "Cast out the slave woman and her son, for the son of the slave woman shall not inherit with the son of the free woman." So, brothers, we are not children of the slave but of the free woman. (Gal. 4:22–31)

In this text, we learn physical Israelites (without faith) are no more the children of promise than Ishmael. Just like Ishmael, physical Israelites (1) are children of the bondwoman, (2) are born slaves, (3) were born of a natural birth, (4) are not the children of promise, and (5) were to be "cast out," for "the son of the slave woman shall not inherit with the son of the free woman."

The future inclusion of the gentiles into God's covenant people, moreover, was prophesied in the Old Testament:

"Sing, O barren one, who did not bear;
  break forth into singing and cry aloud,
  you who have not been in labor!
For the children of the desolate one will be more
  than the children of her who is married," says
the LORD.
"Enlarge the place of your tent,
  and let the curtains of your habitations be stretched
out;
do not hold back; lengthen your cords
  and strengthen your stakes.
For you will spread abroad to the right and to the left,

and your offspring will possess the nations
and will people the desolate cities." (Isa. 54:1–3)

And this prophecy, according to Paul, was speaking of the gentiles who would become the children of Abraham by faith (Gal. 4:27). And in another place, Paul claimed that Hosea prophesied of the addition of the gentiles. In his letter to the Romans, where he speaks of God having mercy on those He has chosen, Paul adds, "Not from the Jews only but also from the Gentiles." And from this Paul cited Hosea who said, "Those who were not my people I will call 'my people,' and her who was not beloved I will call 'beloved.' And in the very place where it was said to them, 'You are not my people,' there they will be called 'sons of the living God.'" (Rom. 9:24–26).

And at the Jerusalem conference, James built a case from the Old Testament Scriptures for accepting the gentiles. According to James, the gentiles were not only to be accepted into God's covenant community, they were to be accepted without requiring circumcision. "And with this the words of the prophets agree," claimed James, "just as it is written, 'After this I will return, and I will rebuild the tent of David that has fallen; I will rebuild its ruins, and I will restore it, that the remnant of mankind may seek the Lord, and all the Gentiles who are called by my name, says the Lord, who makes these things known from of old'" (Acts 15:15–18). "James declares," according to W. J. Grier, "that this rebuilding of the tabernacle of David is now taking place in God's visiting the Gentiles to take out of them a people for His name."[6]

Thus, the Old Testament taught that not all Israel is of real Israel. It also taught that Abraham's children would include the uncircumcised gentiles. This is not replacement theology, nor is it the church (believing Jews and gentiles) commandeering that which was never intended for them. No, this is the actual, literal, and intended fulfillment of the Abrahamic covenant.

The promise was that in Abraham's seed—Jesus Christ—all the nations of the earth shall be blessed (Acts 3:25). The promise was that God would make Abraham the father of many nations (Gen. 17:5). The promised inheritance was not something temporal but something eternal. Thus, the church, as consisting of those who have faith in Christ, is the real Israel of God as taught by the Old and New Testaments.

Conclusion

The first point of amillennialism is the redemptive-historical hermeneutic, which claims that the end of the story helps us understand the beginning of the story. And seeing the New Testament fulfillment of the Abrahamic covenant helps us understand the second point of amillennialism—that not all physical Israel are of dspiritual Israel. Believers who are united to Christ—the

---

[6] W. J. Grier, *The Momentous Event: A Discussion of Scripture Teaching on the Second Advent* (Edinburgh: Banner of Truth, 2018), 46.

church, which consists of Jews and gentiles alike—are the true children of Abraham. Being a physical child of Abraham is not what matters. It's not the law or circumcision that make a person a child of Abraham but faith in Christ. The promises are received by faith alone. And these promises are not merely for believing Jews but extend to believing gentiles. Through Christ, all believers, both Jews and gentiles, are the children of Abraham and heirs to the promises.

3

The Church Is
the Davidic Kingdom

In the first point of amillennialism we learn that the historical and grammatical meaning of a text will be consistent with the overall story line of redemption. For this reason, we understand, in the second point of amillennialism, that the promised children of Abraham are those, and only those, who are united to Christ in faith. Now, in this chapter, as we look at the third point of amillennialism, we will see that the kingdom promised to Abraham, and again promised to David, is (at this present time) a spiritual kingdom.

And this is really at the heart of amillennialism and what separates it from premillennialism and postmillennialism. Amillennialists view the kingdom of God as consisting of only born-again believers without any earthly politicians, military soldiers, or weaponry. Only those who have willingly bowed in submission to the lordship of King Jesus are in the kingdom of heaven and enjoy true unity and peace with God and with one another. And because the kingdom of heaven consists of only believers, it is an everlasting kingdom that has no end. Every other nation will fall, but the kingdom of God, which was not established by human hands, will endure for all eternity. And one day, as with the coming of the new heavens and the new earth, the glory of God will cover the world as the water covers the sea.

To understand the spiritual nature of the kingdom of God in its present state, we need to examine the Abrahamic and Davidic covenants and then look at how the kingdom promised to them was established by Christ, the son of Abraham and the son of David, in the new covenant.

The Kingdom Promised in the Abrahamic Covenant

God called Abraham out of his home country and promised to make him into a great nation (Gen. 12:2). God also promised to give Abraham a people and a territory (Gen. 17:1–8).

After being brought out of Egypt, the physical children of Abraham became a nation (Exodus 19–20). Yet not only did they prove to be characterized by unbelief, rebellion, and idolatry, they experienced only small periods of relative peace. War with other nations and internal fighting among themselves marked the history of Israel. The nation of Israel even divided after the reign of

Solomon, and each division (Israel and Judea) eventually was taken into foreign captivity, never to fully recover.

Surely this wasn't the kingdom that was promised to Abraham. At the very least Abraham was expecting something more glorious and heavenly. By faith Abraham "was looking forward to the city that has foundations, whose designer and builder is God" (Heb. 11:10). Abraham was longing for "a better country, that is, a heavenly one" (v. 16).

The Kingdom
Promised in the Davidic Covenant

The heavenly kingdom promised to the son of Abraham is the same kingdom promised to the son of David. After building himself a magnificent house, King David felt guilty that God was dwelling in a tent. Why should the king dwell in a more glorious house than God? Thus, David determined to build a house—a temple, a dwelling place— for God.

But the interesting thing is that God told David no. Rather than David building God a house, God promised to build David a house:

> I will make for you a great name, like the name of the great ones of the earth. And I will appoint a place for my people Israel and will plant them, so that they may dwell in their own place and be disturbed no more. And violent men shall afflict them no more, as formerly,

from the time that I appointed judges over my people Israel. And I will give you rest from all your enemies. Moreover, the LORD declares to you that the LORD will make you a house. (2 Sam. 7:9–11)

This was not just a house for David but a dwelling place for all the people of God. Wherever this place was supposed to be located, it was going to be a place of safety and peace and rest for the people of God.

David's house not only included a safe dwelling place for God's people, it included a future son. God also promised to give David's son a kingdom. This kingdom would be a kingdom that houses the house and dwelling place of God:

When your days are fulfilled and you lie down with your fathers, I will raise up your offspring after you, who shall come from your body, and I will establish his kingdom. He shall build a house for my name, and I will establish the throne of his kingdom forever. (2 Sam. 7:12–13)

In other words, the house that houses the house of God would be a dwelling place, a kingdom, where God and God's people would dwell together in perfect peace. That is, with God building David a house (a place for David and God's people to dwell in peace) and with the son of David building God a house (a place where God will dwell with His people) the Davidic covenant promised to be a kingdom where God and man dwell together in perfect peace. Thus, this house (where God and man would dwell together) would be built by God and the son of David—the God-man.

Though David wanted to build God a house in his kingdom, God promised to build David a house by giving his son a kingdom that would be a dwelling place for both God and His people. This future kingdom would be an everlasting kingdom of peace where God and His people would dwell harmoniously together forever.

Now this indeed sounds like heaven on earth—where God dwells with His people for all eternity. Regardless, this kingdom far surpasses the kingdoms of this world, having a better dwelling place, a better king, a better peace, and a better temple. Daniel prophesied of the glory and eternity of this kingdom that would come in his interpretation of Nebuchadnezzar's dream:

> And in the days of those kings the God of heaven will set up a kingdom that shall never be destroyed, nor shall the kingdom be left to another people. It shall break in pieces all these kingdoms and bring them to an end, and it shall stand forever, just as you saw that a stone was cut from a mountain by no human hand. (Dan. 2:44–45)

In this we see that the kingdom of God was to be different from all other kingdoms of the world. It was to be established by God. It was to be an everlasting kingdom and a kingdom of rest. It was to be a kingdom and city and house made without human hands. It was to be a kingdom where God would dwell forever with His people in perfect peace.

The Kingdom of God
Established in the New Covenant

Generation after generation of descendants of Abraham would come and go without any heavenly kingdom being established. Though the nation of Israel may have experienced small periods of rest here and there, they were also plagued with various wars throughout their history. They fought continually. They fought not just with other nations but also among themselves. What little peace they enjoyed during the reign of Solomon was soon torn asunder by the division of the kingdom. Eventually, both divisions, because of their unbelief, were utterly defeated and taken into foreign captivity.

Surely whatever measure of peace Israel may have experienced was not the peace promised to David. Surely the house God promised to build David wasn't the house that fell to the Babylonians. And surely the nation of Israel was not the everlasting kingdom that God had promised to give to the son of David.

Regardless, by the time Christ was born, the nation of Israel had long lost any national sovereignty and freedom. But though Israel had proven not to be the everlasting kingdom, God had not forgotten His promise to Abraham and David. In remembrance of His promise, God raised up John the Baptist, the last of the old covenant prophets, to prepare the way for the promised King. John the Baptist came preaching one simple message: "Repent, for the kingdom of heaven is at hand" (Matt. 3:2).

John the Baptist knew that the long-foretold prophecy of Isaiah had been fulfilled in the city of David:

> For to us a child is born,
> to us a son is given;
> and the government shall be upon his shoulder,
> and his name shall be called
> Wonderful Counselor, Mighty God,
> Everlasting Father, Prince of Peace.
> Of the increase of his government and of peace
> there will be no end,
> on the throne of David and over his kingdom,
> to establish it and to uphold it
> with justice and with righteousness
> from this time forth and forevermore.
> The zeal of the LORD of hosts will do this. (Isa. 9:6–7)

With such knowledge, John the Baptist preached the good news of the kingdom of God. And one day, as John was preaching, the seed of Abraham and the son of David came to him to be baptized.

After being baptized by John, Christ began His public ministry preaching the same message as John: "Repent, for the kingdom of heaven is at hand" (Matt. 4:17). Though hundreds of years had passed since God promised Abraham and David a kingdom, the time had finally come for God to fulfill His promise. "The time is fulfilled," proclaimed the Lord, for "the kingdom of God is at hand." It was now time for everyone to "repent and believe in the gospel" (Mark 1:15).

Sadly, many of the leaders of Israel—the scribes and the Pharisees—didn't want such a kingdom. The scribes and Pharisees didn't want a kingdom that was built upon the gospel message. Though they were ready to seize earthly power and control for the nation of Israel, they weren't interested in relinquishing their own perceived power. They wanted to rule without first submitting. They wanted a kingdom but not the gospel of the kingdom. They wanted a king to overcome the Romans but not a king to overcome their sinful hearts. They, like so many who had gone before them, lusted for power and wealth. They were more concerned about liberation from Rome than liberation from Satan, sin, and their sinful flesh. In their pride, they desired to rule the world rather than, in humility, have Christ rule over their lives. They really didn't want peace with God.

In their desire for political freedom, they were eager to appoint themselves a political leader. Some of the Jews longed so much for an earthly ruler that they sought to make Jesus king by force (John 6:15). But Christ had no desire to be an earthly king over the unregenerate. He had no aspiration to lead an insurrection of wicked Jews into battle against the wicked Romans.

Christ had His sights set on a more dangerous enemy. He was not interested in going to war with "flesh and blood, but against the rulers, against the authorities, against the cosmic powers over this present darkness, against the spiritual forces of evil in the heavenly places" (Eph. 6:12). It was the dominion of Satan, not the Roman Empire, that Christ was interested in overcoming. It was Satan, not Caesar, who had enslaved the human race. Christ was not concerned with a little puppet leader in Rome but had His eyes on the Evil One pulling the strings behind the scenes.

Christ came to face down the great red dragon. He came to do war with the very enemy that took down Adam and Eve. He was ready to do battle with the one who has enslaved every soul in every generation since the fall of man. For since the fall, the devil has held the nations of the world in darkness. Every citizen of the world has been blinded by the Prince of Darkness.

For Christ to overcome Satan and rob him of his slaves, He needed something more powerful than an army equipped with shields and swords. Even the best military force would be powerless to overcome the red dragon. A king leading a military force may have conquered Rome, but such an army would have been utterly ineffective in conquering the prince of the power of the air that works in all the children of disobedience (Eph. 2:2).

Christ was uninterested in building a kingdom with unbelievers. The nation of Israel had proven that it was impossible for unbelievers to obey God. It is impossible to legislate sinners into the kingdom of heaven. Laws and legislation and political rule have no power to rule over the conscience. Circumcision of the heart is not administered by laws written on stone. It is the gospel, not the law, that births sinners into the kingdom. The unregenerate will always be at war with God no matter how many righteous laws and restrictions and punishments are placed on them. There can be no peace with the wicked (Isa. 48:22). Light and darkness have nothing in common (2 Cor. 6:14). It would be easier for a lion to lie next to a lamb than for the wicked to lie next to Christ. The kingdom of God cannot be a mixture of regenerate and unregenerate citizens.

For the kingdom of God to come, the kingdom of darkness must fall. For there to be a kingdom of peace, the kingdom must be populated with only those whose sinful hearts have been conquered by the King. Only when sinners are renewed in the inner man by the power of the gospel will there be peace between God and man. This is why Jesus said that one must be born again to enter the kingdom of God (John 3:3). Hence, Jesus didn't come to establish an earthly kingdom. "My kingdom," Christ said, "is not of this world. If my kingdom were of this world, my servants would have been fighting, that I might not be delivered over to the Jews. But my kingdom is not from the world" (John 18:36).

Instead of building a kingdom out of the physical children of Abraham, Christ came to build a kingdom out of the spiritual children of Abraham. But for Christ to establish such a kingdom, Christ had to dethrone the wicked one first. He had to rescue the spiritual children of Abraham from the strong grip of the great deceiver. If He is going to dwell with and in His people, He must cleanse His own elect people first.

Before the outward man can be properly cleansed, the inward man has to be renewed first. Likewise, before the world could be cleansed of its corruption, the power of Satan had to be dismantled. And it was for this reason that the seed of the woman came into the world—to crush the Serpent's head under His feet.

When Christ began to cast out demons in His earthly ministry, He announced that the kingdom of God had arrived (Matt. 12:28). Rather than the kingdom of heaven physically manifesting itself, as some supposed would happen all at once (Luke 19:11), it would come spiritually, one conversion at a time. Unlike other earthly kingdoms, "the kingdom of God," Christ said, "is not coming in ways that can be observed, nor will they say, 'Look, here it is!' or 'There!'" (17:21). Christ is rather building His kingdom slowly by robbing the kingdom of darkness of its citizens. Christ is slowly populating the kingdom of heaven through the new birth.

Though the kingdom of God does not come "in ways that can be observed" (Luke 17:20), those who are born again can see it by faith (John 3:3); and they not only see the kingdom but, by faith, have the kingdom of God within them (Luke 17:21). Together with the law of the kingdom being poured out into their hearts (Rom. 5:5), the King of the kingdom has come to dwell in their hearts by faith (Eph. 3:17).

So, while the nations of the world are waging war against God's anointed, God's anointed are building His kingdom in their very midst. From every nation and people group, Christ is robbing Satan of his prisoners.

Yet before the promised kingdom can be established, the Evil One had to go. Satan's power had to be conquered before the gospel could march through the gates of hell. And this is exactly what Christ did at Calvary. At the very moment when things seemed the darkest, there, on an old rugged cross, the seed of the woman, the heir of Abraham, and the son of David decisively defeated the wicked one. Christ, in His death, at the moment of His weakness, cast out the one who had deceived the world. In His death, He destroyed the one who had the power of death and delivered "all those who through fear of death were subject to lifelong slavery" (Heb. 2:14–15). In so doing, "he disarmed the rulers and authorities and put them to open shame, by triumphing over them in him" (Col. 2:15). Christ Jesus entered the enemy's camp and led captives away from the Prince of Darkness (Eph. 4:8). "He disarmed the rulers and authorities and put them to open shame, by triumphing over them in him" (Col. 2:15).

Though Satan wounded Christ's heel, Christ gave the deathblow to Satan's head. Though Satan continues to roam around like a prowling lion, he is a wounded lion whose power of deception has been greatly impaired. The blanket of darkness that covers the world has been ripped asunder. The light of the gospel is now able to shine through the cracks into the hearts of men. Now that Satan has been "cast out," by Christ by being "lifted up from the earth," Jesus is drawing "all people" to Himself (John 12:31–32).

It was for this reason that Christ came into the world: "To open the eyes that are blind, to bring out the prisoners from the dungeon, from the prison those who sit in darkness" (Isa. 42:7). And now that Satan has been stripped of his power, all things have been placed in subjection to a man, the son of David (Heb. 2:8). And now that all power in heaven and earth has been given to the Son of Man, the Son of Man commands His people to take the gospel to go into all the world (Matt. 28:18–20).

By the authority of Christ, the church has been commissioned to take the gospel of the kingdom to every nation and people group in the world. There is no corner or region that is off limits. The apostle Paul, for example, was sent to the gentiles "to open their eyes, so that they may turn from darkness to light and from the power of Satan to God, that they may receive forgiveness of sins and a place among those who are sanctified by faith" (Acts 26:17–18).

The gospel is no longer restricted to the nation of Israel. Before the cross, God left the gentiles to themselves to grope around in the darkness, but now after the cross, as Paul preached to the Athenians, God commands everyone everywhere to repent of their sins and bow the knee to King Jesus (Acts 17:30).

Ever since His first coming, Christ, through the gospel witness of His people, has been assaulting the gates of hell and retrieving the promised children of Abraham out of every nation, tribe, and people group throughout the world. He will continue to gather His people until the end of the age (Matt. 28:20). Though Satan continues to rage, he is no longer able to stop the light of the gospel from penetrating the hearts of those who God had long ago promised to give to Abraham.

Because of Christ's victory over Satan, the gospel will be victorious over the sinful hearts of His chosen people: "For it is the power of God for salvation to everyone who believes" (Rom. 1:16). The death of Christ secured the victory. The power of the gospel goes out into the dark world like a rider on a white horse "conquering, and to conquer" (Rev. 6:2). Not most but *all* power and authority in heaven and on earth has been given to King Jesus. For Christ either has all power, or He has none at all. Either He is already ruling and reigning, or His first coming was a failure.

But we know that His first coming wasn't a failure. We know that He accomplished all His objectives. And with His victory over the grave, He arose from the dead to take His rightful place on the throne of David; He did this when

He sat down at the right hand of God in heaven. With such power being unleashed on the day of Pentecost, Peter proclaimed that the long-awaited son of David is now seated on the throne of David as Lord and Christ:

> Brothers, I may say to you with confidence about the patriarch David that he both died and was buried, and his tomb is with us to this day. Being therefore a prophet, and knowing that God had sworn with an oath to him that he would set one of his descendants on his throne, he foresaw and spoke about the resurrection of the Christ, that he was not abandoned to Hades, nor did his flesh see corruption. This Jesus God raised up, and of that we all are witnesses. Being therefore exalted at the right hand of God and having received from the Father the promise of the Holy Spirit, he has poured out this that you yourselves are seeing and hearing. For David did not ascend into the heavens, but he himself says,

> "The Lord said to my Lord,
> 'Sit at my right hand,
>   until I make your enemies your footstool.'"

> Let all the house of Israel therefore know for certain that God has made him both Lord and Christ, this Jesus whom you crucified. (Acts 2:29–36)

Conclusion

The son of David is not only on the throne of David, He will and must continue to reign on David's throne until He has conquered all His enemies (1 Cor. 15:25). Yet, before He returns to defeat the last enemy, death, He must continue to subdue His own people's hearts by rescuing them from the coils of the serpent. And He must continue to reign until He has gathered every last promised child of Abraham into the everlasting kingdom.

And when He has finished building His kingdom by populating it with the children of Abraham, He will subdue the wicked by destroying and purging the world with fire. Then, when everything is perfectly restored, Christ will deliver the kingdom to His Father as a spotless bride, holy and without blemish. Afterward, all tears will be wiped away, and Christ Jesus will dwell with His people forever in the Land of Promise—the new heavens and the new earth. And this leads us to the fourth point of amillennialism.

4

The New Earth
Is the Promised Land

To say that the kingdom of God is spiritual and heavenly in nature is not to say that the kingdom will not one day be physical in nature. Though Abraham, by faith, was looking for a heavenly city, it was the world that God promised to give him (Rom. 4:13). He was not only promised the land he walked on, Abraham was promised everything to the north, to the south, to the east, and to the west as an *everlasting* inheritance (Gen. 13:14–15). Thus, it would seem that the heavenly and eternal city that Abraham was looking to inherit was to be located one day on the earth.

Well, at least it appears this way when we consider the fact that the promised land was to be a physical inheritance: "for all the land that you see I will give to you and to your offspring forever" (v. 15). Though it may be argued that this inheritance was to remain in Abraham's family from one generation to the next until the end of the age, there is more reason to believe that this promise has yet to be fulfilled. There are eight reasons to believe that the promised land is the new heavens and the new earth.

One, the promised land was physical land—the very land that Abraham saw with his own eyes: "for all the land that you see I will give to you." Again, God said to Abraham: "I am the LORD who brought you out from Ur of the Chaldeans to give you this land to possess" (Gen. 15:7).

Two, the promise was to be given to Abraham, not just to Abraham's children: "For all the land that you see I will give *to you* and to your children" (Gen. 13:15). The promise was not that God would give the land to Abraham vicariously through his children but that God would give it to both Abraham and to Abraham's children to enjoy.

Three, Abraham has yet to inherit any of this land. The only land that Abraham owned was the small plot he bought (not received or inherited from God) from Ephron in Machpelah to bury his wife Sarah (Gen. 23:10–16). Concerning the promised land, Abraham lived and died without receiving one acre of it. The Bible says that he wandered his whole life as a stranger in a foreign land without receiving the things that were promised to him (Heb. 11:13).

Four, the land was to be an everlasting inheritance: "for all the land that you see I will give to you and to your offspring *forever*." In another place it says,

> He remembers his covenant forever,
>> the word that he commanded, for a thousand
> generations,
> the covenant that he made with Abraham,
>> his sworn promise to Isaac,
> which he confirmed to Jacob as a statute,
>> to Israel as an *everlasting covenant*,
> saying, "To you I will give the land of Canaan
>> as your portion for an inheritance." (Ps. 105:8–11)

Whenever Abraham inherits the land, it will never be taken away from him. When Abraham inherits the land, he will dwell in it forever.

Five, not only does this strongly imply that the heavenly city is an everlasting city but that Abraham would have eternal life, or otherwise he couldn't enjoy it *forever*.

Six, this infers that the children of Abraham, who also inherit the land, will live forever. Together with his children Abraham will enjoy life forever in the Land of Promise. And like Abraham, all the true children of Abraham have, by faith, turned their backs on this world and have placed their hope in a more lasting home:

> For people who speak thus make it clear that they are seeking a homeland. If they had been thinking of that land from which they had gone out, they would have had opportunity to return. But as it is, they desire a better country, that is, a heavenly one. Therefore, God is not ashamed to be called their God, for he has prepared for them a city. (Heb. 11:14–16)

Seven, if the children of Abraham are to enjoy the promised land forever, then these heirs must be Abraham's children by faith. For it is only those who have faith, as with Abraham, who will have eternal life. As explained by Paul, "for the promise to Abraham and his offspring that he would be heir of the world did not come through the law but through the righteousness of faith" (Rom. 4:13).

Eight, and consequently, for the promised land to be the earth, the term *promised land* must refer to the new heavens and the new earth—a place where only righteousness and righteous people dwell (2 Peter 3:13). And does not the Bible speak of the new creation as the everlasting abode of the children of God (Rom. 8:21)? And did not Jesus say that the meek shall inherit the earth (Matt. 5:5)?

Thus, the idea that the new earth is the promised land is the fourth point of amillennialism.

Partial Fulfillment

If the new creation is the promised land, the promises of the Abrahamic covenant have only been partially fulfilled. We have seen, in the third point of amillennialism, that the kingdom of God has already been inaugurated in the hearts of Abraham's spiritual children. The kingdom of God is currently spiritual. In some respects, much of the Abrahamic covenant is already realized. Yet, if the new earth is the promised land, there is still something missing. We, as Abraham's spiritual children, by faith are awaiting the physical resurrection and the re-creation of the new heavens and the new earth. Until then, we wander in this world as pilgrims and strangers.

Already but Not Yet

This partial fulfillment of the Abrahamic covenant is often explained by the "already but not yet" conception of the kingdom of God. For instance, the kingdom of God has *already* been inaugurated but *not yet* consummated. Though the fullness of the Old Testament promises will not be realized until after the second coming of Christ, the first fruits of the age to come have already sprouted in the lives of believers.

George Ladd explained it this way: "The early church found itself living in a tension between realization and expectation—between 'already' and 'not yet.' The age of fulfillment has come; the day of consummation stands yet in the future."[7]

To better understand the *already but not yet* (partial) fulfillment of the Old Testament promises, it is important to see that (1) there is a two-phase fulfillment of the kingdom of God and (2) there are two comings of Christ, (3) two ages, and (4) two kingdoms.

---

[7] George Ladd, *A Theology of the New Testament* (Grand Rapids: Eerdmans, 1993), 368.

The Two-Stage Fulfillment
(Spiritual and Physical) of the Kingdom of God

The already but not yet conception of the kingdom implies that there is a two-stage fulfillment of the kingdom of God that was promised to Abraham and David. The kingdom of God was inaugurated at the first coming of Christ, though it has not been physically consummated in the new heavens and the new earth, which will take place at Christ's second coming. The citizens of heaven have already received eternal life, though their bodies remain under the curse of the fall. Christ has already conquered and subdued the hearts of His people, but He is yet to fully conquer and subdue the nations and remove the curse that holds the creation in subjection.

According to Paul, all creation is groaning along with those of us who have the firstfruits of the Spirit. Paul explained that we are groaning inwardly together "as we wait eagerly for adoption as sons, the redemption of our bodies" (Rom. 8:19–23). Though we have been given some of the promises, that is, the firstfruits of the Spirit, the full inheritance of Abraham is still awaiting us.

Although the inner man has been redeemed, the body is yet to be glorified. Likewise, though some of the promises of Abraham are coming to fruition, such as God calling out the children of Abraham from every nation, the complete inheritance, such as the promised land, has yet to materialize. The kingdom of God is now spiritual, but it will one day also be physical—with the coming of the new heavens and the new earth where only righteousness dwells.

"Because the kingdom is both present and future," Anthony Hoekema claims, "we may say that the kingdom is now hidden to all except those who have faith in Christ, but that someday it shall be totally revealed, so that even its enemies will finally have to recognize its presence and bow before its rule."[8] The first fruits of heaven have sprouted in the hearts of believers in this present evil age, though the full harvest has yet to be fully realized in the eternal state of glory.

In the eternal state of glory, heaven and earth will be perfectly united under the reign of Christ (Eph. 1:10; Col. 1:20). When all evil is uprooted and the wicked and this present evil world is destroyed with the re-creation of the new earth, God will then dwell with man in perfect unity and peace forever. Truly, heaven will fill the earth "with the knowledge of the glory of the LORD as the waters cover the sea" (Hab. 2:14).

At that time, the Abrahamic covenant will be fully realized. Abraham and his children, who have been drawn out from every nation and people group of the world, will dwell in the Land of Promise forever. As Hoekema asserts,

> The Kingdom of God, therefore, is to be understood as
> the reign of God dynamically active in human history

[8] Anthony A. Hoekema, *The Bible and the Future* (Grand Rapids: Eerdmans, 1979), 53.

through Jesus Christ, the purpose of which is the redemption of God's people from sin and from demonic powers, and the final establishment of the new heavens and the new earth. It means that the great drama of the history of salvation has been inaugurated, and that the new age has been ushered in. The kingdom must not be understood as merely the salvation of a certain individual or even the reign of God in the hearts of his people; it means nothing less than the reign of God over his entire created universe."[9]

Two Comings of Christ

The two-phase fulfillment of Old Testament promises corresponds to the two-phase coming of Christ. The Old Testament prophesied that the coming King would establish both peace and justice. The Old Testament spoke of the day of the Lord as a day of wrath for the enemies of God's people (Joel 2:1–2; Amos 5:18–20; Zeph. 1:14–15) and a day of mercy for God's people (Isaiah 53).

The Coming of Christ Was to Be a Day of Judgment

According to Zephaniah, the day of the Lord was to be a day of judgment for all the inhabitants of the earth:

"I will utterly sweep away everything
    from the face of the earth," declares the LORD.
"I will sweep away man and beast;

---

[9] Hoekema, 45.

I will sweep away the birds of the heavens
and the fish of the sea,
and the rubble with the wicked.
I will cut off mankind
from the face of the earth," declares the LORD. . . .

The great day of the LORD is near,
near and hastening fast;
the sound of the day of the LORD is bitter;
the mighty man cries aloud there.
A day of wrath is that day,
a day of distress and anguish,
a day of ruin and devastation,
a day of darkness and gloom,
a day of clouds and thick darkness,
a day of trumpet blast and battle cry
against the fortified cities
and against the lofty battlements.

I will bring distress on mankind,
so that they shall walk like the blind,
because they have sinned against the LORD;
their blood shall be poured out like dust,
and their flesh like dung.
Neither their silver nor their gold
shall be able to deliver them
on the day of the wrath of the LORD.
In the fire of his jealousy,
all the earth shall be consumed;
for a full and sudden end
he will make of all the inhabitants of the earth.
(Zeph. 1:2–3, 14–18)

According to the prophet Isaiah, the Lord was to come in judgment:

> Behold, the day of the LORD comes,
>   cruel, with wrath and fierce anger,
> to make the land a desolation
>   and to destroy its sinners from it.
> For the stars of the heavens and their constellations
>   will not give their light;
> the sun will be dark at its rising,
>   and the moon will not shed its light.
> I will punish the world for its evil,
>   and the wicked for their iniquity. (Isa. 13:9–11)

The Coming of Christ Was to Be a Day of Mercy

Also, according to Isaiah, the Lord was to come with the good news of salvation:

> I am the LORD; I have called you in righteousness;
>   I will take you by the hand and keep you;
> I will give you as a covenant for the people,
>   a light for the nations,
>   to open the eyes that are blind,
> to bring out the prisoners from the dungeon,
>   from the prison those who sit in darkness. (Isa. 42:6–7)

A Day of Wrath and a Day of Mercy

Thus, in the Old Testament, both peace and judgment are connected to the coming of the King. Not only does the Old Testament speak of the Messiah as the person who will triumph over His enemies and bring the nations into subjection to the people of God (Zeph. 3:8), it speaks of the same Messiah as the suffering servant (Isa. 53:7). The Messiah was to come to serve and suffer as well as to rule and reign. The Messiah was not only to bring peace to the nations, He was to reign over the nations in judgment. In Him all the nations of the earth were to be blessed, but by Him all the nations of the earth were also to be condemned. He was to bring both joy and woe to the world.

But how can Christ do both at His appearing? How can He bring healing and destruction to the nations?

Not One but Two Comings

Though it may be hard to see from reading the Old Testament how Christ was to bring both joy and woe to the world at His appearing, by reading the New Testament we learn that Christ's appearing actually takes place in two phases—His first coming and His second coming. What appeared to be a single event is actually, according to the New Testament, a single event separated into two phases. Or, as William Cox states, "These are not in reality two separate events, but rather two steps in one plan. The two comings complement each other, and one could not be complete without the other."[10] "With characteristic prophetic perspective," Hoekema suggests, "the Old Testament prophets intermingled items relating to the first

---

[10] William Cox, *Biblical Studies in Final Things* (Phillipsburg, NJ: P&R, 1966), 15.

coming of Christ with items relating to Christ's second coming. Not until New Testament times would it be revealed that what was thought of in Old Testament days as one coming of the Messiah would be fulfilled in two stages: a first and a second coming."[11]

At His first coming, Christ suffered and brought good news to the world. At His second coming, Christ will bring woe and judgment to the world. His first coming is a coming in peace. His second coming is a coming in judgment. The sign of His first coming was a harmless "baby wrapped in swaddling cloths and lying in a manger" (Luke 2:12). The sign of a manger was a sign that God has come in peace. The sign of Christ's second coming will be a fierce warrior riding into battle to bring recompense on all who have not accepted His terms of peace. He suffered under the hands of the wicked in His first appearing, but He will conquer and reign over the wicked at His second appearing.

The two-phase fulfillment of the coming of Christ can be seen when John the Baptist began to doubt that Jesus was indeed the Christ. John the Baptist was expecting the Messiah to rule over the nations of the earth. He was looking for the kingdom of God to bring the kingdoms of this world into subjection. Yet, rather than the righteous ruling over the unrighteous, the righteous were being imprisoned by the unrighteous. In other words, John the Baptist was not expecting for his ministry to end the way it

[11] Hoekema, *The Bible and the Future*, 12.

did. He did not think introducing the King to the world would end with his head on a platter. And with his expectations not being met, he began to doubt that Jesus was the Messiah. Maybe he had been mistaken. With such doubt, he sent his disciples to question Jesus: "Are you the one who is to come, or shall we look for another?" (Luke 7:19).

To reassure John that He was the promised Messiah, Jesus responded by quoting the well-known prophecy of Isaiah: "Go and tell John what you have seen and heard: the blind receive their sight, the lame walk, lepers are cleansed, and the deaf hear, the dead are raised up, the poor have good news preached to them. And blessed is the one who is not offended by me" (vv. 22–23). What is interesting is that Jesus didn't finish the prophecy. He stopped mid-sentence. The passage that Christ cited from Isaiah actually goes on to speak of Christ judging the nations: "The Spirit of the Lord GOD is upon me, because the LORD has anointed me to bring good news to the poor; he has sent me to bind up the brokenhearted, to proclaim liberty to the captives, and the opening of the prison to those who are bound; to proclaim the year of the LORD's favor, and the day of vengeance of our God" (Isa. 61:1–2).

Yet the Lord purposefully stopped before mentioning "the day of vengeance of our God." For the day of good news, healing, liberty, and favor is a different day than "the day of vengeance." So, the Lord's response to John the Baptist was "Yes, I am the Christ." Though He was not yet taking vengeance on the unrighteous, He was currently fulfilling the first part of the prophecy. In other words, this was the day of healing and suffering, not the day of vengeance and wrath.

What is more interesting is that the ministry of John the Baptist was distinctly connected with the first phase of Christ's coming. According to Malachi, unless God had sent John the Baptist ahead of Christ to prepare the way of the Lord, the day of vengeance would have prevented there being a day of healing and suffering. If God didn't separate His coming into two stages, there would not have been a people gathered out of all the nations before judgment came upon the nations. "Behold, I will send you Elijah the prophet before the great and awesome day of the LORD comes. And he will turn the hearts of fathers to their children and the hearts of children to their fathers, lest I come and strike the land with a decree of utter destruction" (Mal. 4:5–6).

For this reason, William Cox states, "It is because of the success of the first coming of our Lord that Christians have such great confidence as they look forward to his glorious appearing."[12] According to Hoekema,

> What is unique about New Testament eschatology is that it expects a future consummation of God's purposes based on Christ's victory in the past. George Ladd makes this point: "Its [the church's] witness to God's victory in the future is based on a victory already achieved in

---

[12] Cox, *Biblical Studies in Final Things*, 15–16.

history. It proclaims not merely hope, but a hope based on events in history and its own experience."[13]

Thus, it is clear that what often appeared in the Old Testament to be a single appearing of the Messiah is actually, according to the New Testament, divided into two comings. This is crucial because the kingdom comes with the coming of the King. Wherever the King is, there is the kingdom. And seeing that Christ's appearing takes place in two phases, the kingdom of God comes in two phases. In the first coming, the King gathers His people from out of the nations; in the second coming, the King will conquer the nations. In the first coming, Christ established His spiritual reign within the hearts of His people; in the second coming, Christ will establish His physical reign in a perfectly restored universe.

"There is, therefore," according to Sam Storms, "a dual manifestation of the kingdom of God corresponding to the two comings of Christ himself." Storms goes on to state, "He *first* appeared in obscurity and humility, to suffer and die for the vindication of God's righteousness and the salvation of his people. . . . He will yet appear a *second* time in visible power and greatness to deliver the earth from the curse of sin, to glorify his people, and to establish his sovereign rule forever in the consummated splendor of the new heavens and new earth."[14]

---

[13] Hoekema, *The Bible and the Future*, 21.
[14] Storms, *Kingdom Come*, 340–41.

Two Ages

These two phases of the kingdom of God (phase one, inauguration, and phase two, consummation) can be seen in the two ages (or major time periods) that are spoken about in the New Testament: *this present evil age* and *the age to come* (Gal. 1:4; Eph. 1:21). The first coming introduced the age to come, and the second coming will end this present evil age. But what are these two ages or time periods?

The Present Evil Age

This present evil age, according to Scripture, is the time period that spans from the fall of Adam until the second coming of Christ (Matt. 28:20). The present evil age is the time period in which darkness, bondage, unrighteousness, sin, and death reign over the earth. The present evil age will endure as long as there is sin in the world.

According to Christ, unbelievers are born into this fallen world as the "children of this age" (Luke 20:34 CSB), and according to Paul, the children of this age are held captive to the power of this age (Gal. 1:4–5). This present evil age, consequently, is the reign of the kingdom of darkness over the people and the nations of this age (Rev. 18:3).

The Age to Come

If this present evil age is the time period in which evil dwells on the earth, then *the age to come* is the time period in which righteousness will dwell on the earth (2 Peter 3:13). And though the age to come will not be fully realized until the creation of the new earth, where only righteousness dwells, the firstfruits of the age to come have already been introduced in this present evil age. Since the first coming of Christ, as demonstrated by His own resurrection, the power of the age to come has entered the world. And with the power of the resurrected Christ continuing to transform dead sinners into new creations (2 Cor. 5:17), the power of the age to come continues to operate in this present evil age.

The power of the age to come, therefore, is being manifested on the earth within the hearts of believers (Titus 2:11–13). Those who have been united, by faith, to the King of Glory have "tasted the goodness of the word of God and the powers of the age to come" (Heb. 6:5). They have been delivered from the domain and kingdom of darkness and transferred into the kingdom of God's dear Son (Col. 1:13). In other words, the power and blessings of the age to come have already commenced in part within the lives of believers (Luke 17:20–21; John 18:36).

Inaugurated Eschatology

The inauguration of the power of the age to come in this present evil age is a foretaste of heaven. It is a portion of the power, righteousness, and glory of the eternal state. Anthony Hoekema identified this as *inaugurated eschatology*. "Inaugurated eschatology," according to Hoekema, "implies that eschatology has indeed begun, but is by no means finished."[15] Inaugurated eschatology is the resurrected Christ introducing within the lives of His followers the firstfruits of the eternal state (i.e., the *eschaton*).

Overlapping Ages

Though the power of the future has already been inaugurated, the power of darkness is not a thing of the past. The power and dominion of this present evil age still has a grip on all the children of darkness. This has several implications:

First, this implies that though the power of the kingdom of heaven is *already* present within the lives of believers, it is *not yet* manifested over the kingdoms of this world. The world knows nothing of the life, power, freedom, and peace of the kingdom of God. The nations and rulers of this age remain in darkness and under the dominion of Satan.

Second, this implies that the present evil age and the age to come are currently overlapping. Between the first and second comings of Christ, the two ages run side by side. Though the age to come has been introduced, the present evil age has yet to fully expire.

And third, this implies, according to W. J. Grier, "The heavenly world and the earthly sphere are now parallel states, to both of which the believer belongs."[16] In other words, believers find themselves living in two kingdoms at

---

[15] Hoekema, *The Bible and the Future*, 18.
[16] Grier, *The Momentous Event*, 54.

the same time. On the one hand, believers are citizens of the kingdom of heaven and have already experienced the power of the age to come. On the other hand, believers still live in this fallen world and experience the ongoing effects and influences of the kingdom of darkness.

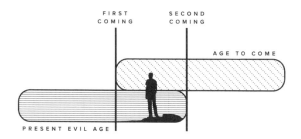

Believers experience the tension between the two ages in two ways: (1) within their own lives, and (2) within the world in which they live.

First, from within their own lives, believers experience the evil effects of this present evil age within their decaying bodies while they experience the redeeming effects of the age to come within their renewed minds and hearts. Not only do believers battle sinful desires, they feel the ongoing effects of sin in their failing bodies. Though their inward man is renewed day by day in the image of Christ, their outward man is perishing (2 Cor. 4:16). Therefore, because "our citizenship is in heaven," the apostle Paul said, "we await a Savior, the Lord Jesus Christ, who will transform our lowly body to be like his glorious body, by the power that enables him even to subject all things to himself" (Phil. 3:20–21).

Second, we experience the tension between the two ages as we live as both citizens of heaven and of this world. This present evil age will not pass away until the second coming of Christ. Until then, we have been sent into the world as sheep amid wolves (Matt. 10:16). Though we live in this world, we are not of this world. And though we are not of this world, we still live in this world for the time being. And because we are not of this world in which we live, we are hated by this world (John 15:19; 17:16). We, as Christ foretold, are hated by all nations (Matt. 24:9).

Yet, we who believe "consider that the sufferings of this present time are not worth comparing with the glory that is to be revealed" in us (Rom. 8:18), "for [our] light momentary affliction is preparing for us an eternal weight of glory beyond all comparison" (2 Cor. 4:17).

Thus, we groan along with creation under the persecution and curse of this present evil age. As Paul said,

> For the creation waits with eager longing for the revealing of the sons of God. For the creation was subjected to futility, not willingly, but because of him who subjected it, in hope that the creation itself will be set free from its bondage to corruption and obtain the freedom of the glory of the children of God. For we know that the whole creation has been groaning together in the pains of childbirth until now. And not only the creation, but we ourselves, who have the

firstfruits of the Spirit, groan inwardly as we wait eagerly for adoption as sons, the redemption of our bodies. (Rom. 8:19–23)

Two Kingdoms (Jurisdictions)

Until that great day when this present evil age comes to a destructive end, we who believe live as strangers and pilgrims and foreigners and exiles in this world (Heb. 11:13; 1 Peter 2:11). Though we were once strangers and foreigners to the kingdom of heaven (Eph. 2:19), we are now citizens of heaven and strangers to this world (Phil. 3:20). Since this world is no longer our home, we, like Abraham, are looking for a more permanent city to call our home (Heb. 11:10).

During our short stay, as we await to enter our eternal abode, we are called to live here below as ambassadors of the kingdom of heaven. We have been sent by our King to represent Him and His glorious kingdom in this fallen world (2 Cor. 5:20). We are called to be a light in the darkness. We have been sent into the enemy's territory to preach the gospel of the kingdom and to rescue the dying.

While we are temporary residents of this world we are under dual jurisdictions. We are called to obey two distinct authorities. We are citizens of the kingdom of heaven and earthly citizens of the kingdoms and nations of this world. David VanDrunen explains it this way:

Christians are citizens of two distinct kingdoms, both of which are ordained of God and under his law, yet exist for different purposes, have different functions, and operate according to different rules. In their capacity as citizens of the spiritual kingdom of Christ, Christians insist upon non-violence and the ways of peace, refusing to bear arms on behalf of his kingdom. In their capacity as citizens of the civil kingdom, they participate as necessary in the coercive work of the state, bearing arms on its behalf when occasion warrants. As citizens of the spiritual kingdom they have no patriotic allegiance to any earthly nation. But as citizens of the civil kingdom a healthy patriotism is certainly possible.[17]

Because of our dual citizenship, we are to "render to Caesar the things that are Caesar's, and to God the things that are God's" (Mark 12:17). As pilgrims in this world, we are called to both fear God and to honor the king (1 Peter 2:17). We are called to pay our taxes to the state (Matt. 22:21) and freely give our offerings to the church (1 Cor. 9:11). As citizens of this world, we are called to richly enjoy all things (1 Tim. 6:17). As citizens of heaven, we are called to lay up our treasures in heaven and seek first the kingdom of God (Matt. 6:20, 33). In our submission to the Lord, we are called to be in subjection "to every human institution, whether it be to the emperor as supreme, or to

---

[17] David VanDrunen, *Natural Law and the Two Kingdoms* (Grand Rapids: Eerdmans, 2010), 13.

governors as sent by him to punish those who do evil and to praise those who do good" (1 Peter 2:13–14).

Our greater loyalty, however, is to the kingdom of heaven. When the commands of man violate the commands of God, we are called to civil disobedience. We "must obey God rather than men" (Acts 5:29).

This greater loyalty to God, even when it leads us to civil disobedience, is a benefit to society. Just because the ship is sinking, does not mean we are called to abandon ship. Our love for Christ and the Great Commission compel us to go into the world rather than retreating from society. Our Christian values influence how we vote, and they mandate that we are productive citizens of this world. Among many other things, we stand for the traditional family, and we stand against abortion. Our desire to love our neighbors constrains us to be active members of society and personally help those in need, pray for our rulers, and do what we can to promote justice and peace in this present evil age.

The culture as a whole is externally benefited by the inward and personal transformation that takes place within the individual followers of Christ. The more a society consists of those who have been born again, the more that society is impacted for good. No doubt, many temporal benefits follow the spread and reception of the gospel. We are indeed the salt of the earth (Matt. 5:13). If nothing else, if it weren't for the redeemed, there would be nothing preventing God from destroying the world.

The gospel changes societies at the individual level. The gospel is not designed for political revolution but for reaching the lost with the hope of eternal life. Unless sinners submit to the gospel of the kingdom, they have no lasting hope. God is not interested in moralizing the wicked. God has not promised to sanctify the culture or to redeem earthly governments, nor is He concerned with Christianizing the wicked with the false hope of external morality.

Though the gospel can lift the community, it can nonetheless bring hostilities and divisions. As Kim Riddlebarger points out,

> The advance of God's kingdom, while inevitable, does not guarantee that evil in society will abate as the kingdom advances. In fact, the presence of God's kingdom guarantees conflict with the forces of evil. . . . wherever Christ's kingdom advances, Christians must do combat with our three great enemies—the world, the flesh, and the devil. The Christian hope is that one day the kingdom will be consummated when all evil will be crushed by the Lamb, but not before. [18]

The Two Kingdoms Are Incompatible

Therefore, though Christians live in both kingdoms, these two kingdoms remain distinct jurisdictions. Like oil and water, the kingdom of darkness and the kingdom of heaven

---

[18] Kim Riddlebarger, *A Case for Amillennialism: Understanding the End Times* (Grand Rapids: Baker, 2003), 110.

are incompatible. Light and darkness have nothing in common (2 Cor. 6:14). The church, as it has been redeemed of God, and the state, as it remains under the influence of darkness, have not been united by the Lord. Though Christ rules them both, the state has no jurisdiction over the church, and the church has no jurisdiction over the state.

Yes, every square inch of this universe currently belongs to the rule of Christ, but not all of it has bowed the knee to Christ. Though He sovereignly rules over Satan and the kingdoms of this world, Christ's rule is only embraced by those who have been born again. His kingdom doesn't come without His will being done (Matt. 6:10).

Only Abraham's spiritual children have submitted to the lordship of Christ. Only those who have tasted the powers of the age to come have God's protection from the wrath to come. Only those who are united to Christ have found peace and liberty under His leadership and have experienced the liberating power of the age to come. Thus, the kingdom of heaven, in this present evil age, will not expand beyond those who are united by faith to the King.

And though every political leader, governor, and king will have to give an account to King Jesus, there is no divine promise that political leaders will govern justly.

The State Has No Jurisdiction over the Church

Though political power may influence external behavior for the good (which is a common grace and a good thing), political power cannot undo the kingdom of darkness that lies within the hearts of those enslaved to the ruler of this present evil age. The theocracy of the Jewish state in the Old Testament proved that even the legislation issued by God cannot establish the kingdom of heaven on earth. Laws on stone do not change hearts of stone. In 1523, Martin Luther stated it this way:

> The worldly government has laws which extend no farther than to life and property and outward affairs on earth. For over the soul God can and will let no one rule but Himself. Therefore, where the worldly authority arrogates to prescribe laws for soul, it encroaches upon God's government and only misleads souls and corrupts them. We want to make this crystal clear so that everyone will grasp it, and that our fine noblemen, the princes and bishops, will see what fools they are when they seek coercing people with their laws and commandments into believing this or that.[19]

"Faith is a free act," Luther went on to say, "to which no one can be forced"[20] Only those who, by the power of the Holy Spirit, willingly come to Christ can come at all. Freedom of the conscience and the separation of church and state are basic tenets of New Testament Christianity.

It can be argued, moreover, that the kingdom of God thrived better under Roman persecution than it did after

---

[19] Martin Luther, *On Worldly Authority: To What Extent It Should be Obeyed* (n.p.: Glocktower, 2016), 35-36.
[20] Luther, *On Worldly Authority*, 38.

Rome Romanized Christianity. One of the most dreadful attacks against the kingdom of God happened when Christianity became the state religion in the Middle Ages.

Not that hostilities and persecution are to be desired, but the advancement and perpetuity of the kingdom of God is not dependent on the aid and assistance of any earthly government. Christ has promised to build His church with or without the protection of the state. Often the church grows faster under state-sponsored persecution. One thing is for certain—just as the kingdom of God outlasted the Roman Empire, it will outlast every other national power (Dan. 2:44).

In the end, civil authorities have no power to dictate the conscience because they have no power to police and punish the conscience. The best that earthly governments can do, even if they are led by Christians, is to restrain evil and punish evildoers (1 Peter 2:14).

The Church Has No Jurisdiction over the State

In the same way that the state has no jurisdiction over the church, the church has no business carrying out its mission by the use of the earthly weapons of this world (2 Cor. 10:4). Just as Christ did not attempt to establish His kingdom through political force (John 18:36), The church should not be deceived into thinking they can expand God's kingdom through political and social revolutions. Taking over the state is not the objective of the church. Political activism, marches, protests, and rallies are not the keys to the kingdom of heaven. "For we do not wrestle against flesh and blood, but against the rulers, against the authorities, against the cosmic powers over this present darkness, against the spiritual forces of evil in the heavenly places" (Eph. 6:12).

Though the state is under the rule of Christ, Christ has not promised to redeem the state. There is no way to rid the culture of sin without ridding the culture of sinners. And as long as unredeemed sinners exist in this world, the world will remain under the influence and bondage of sin. That which has been defaced by sin cannot be refurbished through cultural restoration. It is not refurbishing but a re-creation that the world needs. Sinners must die to sin, self, and this world and be reborn by the Holy Spirit before they can enter the kingdom of God (John 3:3).

Likewise, the world (and all that is in it—nations, cultures, and philosophies) must be destroyed with fire and be totally re-created before it will be liberated from bondage and the corruption of the fall. The world needs more than remodeling; it needs to be burned down and re-created into something altogether new.

The only eternal hope for this world is the gospel message that has been entrusted to the ambassadors of the kingdom of heaven. For this reason, the great hope is not the restoration of this present evil age by social reforms and legislative laws but that God would continue to call out a people for Himself from out of every nation and people group of this world before it is destroyed.[21]

The Union of Earth (Physical) and Heaven (Spiritual)

According to the Scriptures, the kingdom of darkness will not come to an end until the glorious return of the King. The nations will not be conquered and subdued and judged until the King's glorious return. It is only then that the King of Kings "will rule them with a rod of iron, as when earthen pots are broken in pieces" (Rev. 2:26–27; 18:1–10).

Then, at Christ's second coming the kingdom of heaven, which was inaugurated with the first coming of Christ, will be consummated. The first coming introduced the powers and blessings of the age to come into the hearts of Abraham's spiritual children. Christ came the first time to bring good news to the nations. In that, He came to call sinners to repentance and to call out Abraham's spiritual offspring from every nation, tribe, and people group. He came to establish the kingdom of heaven within the hearts of believers so that Abraham would have an offspring as numerous as the stars to fill the new earth with the glory and knowledge of God. In short, the first coming was to call out God's people and prepare them for His second coming.

---

[21] To learn more about the nature and relationship between the two kingdoms, see David VanDrunen, *Living in God's Two Kingdoms: A Biblical Vision for Christianity and Culture* (Wheaton, IL: Crossway, 2010).

Likewise, though the kingdom of God is currently invisible to unbelievers, one day it will, with the new heavens and the new earth, fill the physical world with the glory of God. This will be a new world where only believers and righteousness dwell. Only when this present evil age comes to an end, and only when all the nations of world and all the wicked are destroyed with fire, will God unite our new bodies with our redeemed souls and make heaven and earth one. Then the promise that the son of David, the God-man, would build a dwelling place for the people of God will be wholly fulfilled, and when Christ returns, God and man will dwell in perfect peace in the promised land forever.

> Then I saw a new heaven and a new earth, for the first heaven and the first earth had passed away, and the sea was no more. And I saw the holy city, new Jerusalem, coming down out of heaven from God, prepared as a bride adorned for her husband. And I heard a loud voice from the throne saying, "Behold, the dwelling place of God is with man. He will dwell with them, and they will be his people, and God himself will be with them as their God. He will wipe away every tear from their eyes, and death shall be no more, neither shall there be mourning, nor crying, nor pain anymore, for the former things have passed away." (Rev. 21:1–4)

The Abrahamic covenant will be fully realized when Abraham and all his spiritual offspring inherit the earth as an everlasting possession to dwell forever in the presence of God:

> After this I looked, and behold, a great multitude that no one could number, from every nation, from all tribes and peoples and languages, standing before the throne and before the Lamb, clothed in white robes, with palm branches in their hands, and crying out with a loud voice, "Salvation belongs to our God who sits on the throne, and to the Lamb!" (Rev. 7:9–10)

Not Spiritualizing Literal Promises

This is not the spiritualization of literal promises. This is not denying the importance of the physical fulfillment of the Old Testament promises. Just because there is a spiritual fulfillment first does not mean there will not one day be a physical fulfillment afterward. Just because the new birth takes place before the new body is received and the heavenly reign before the earthly reign does not mean the promises are not going to be physically fulfilled. As a general rule, the promises of the Old Testament have been fulfilled *spiritually* in the first coming, and they will be fulfilled *physically* in the second coming.

We do not have to choose between literal and spiritual fulfillments, as if the promises have to be one or the other. This is not the issue at all. Rather, the issue is between *temporal* and *eternal* fulfillments. The question we need to answer is this: Were the promises of the Old Testament temporal or eternal promises? Now, *this* is the issue.

The inheritance that Abraham passed on to Isaac was a temporal inheritance. In fact, every physical thing that is enjoyed on this side of the second coming of Christ, in this present age, is temporal. Everything in this world will come to an end. There are no earthly possessions that will be carried with us into the age to come. Everything will be destroyed with fire on that great and fearful day of the Lord. But the heirs and the inheritance of Abraham, which comes by faith, will last forever.

Abraham, though he currently rules and reigns with Christ in heaven, will one day be resurrected in his new body and will dwell in the land forever with all his children. Though his earthly possessions, which were passed on to Isaac and Jacob, have passed away, the inheritance God promised to Abraham and his spiritual children cannot pass away. Thus, anything short of an eternal inheritance falls short of being the intended fulfillment of the Abrahamic covenant.

Conclusion

In conclusion, the new earth is the promised land. Though the kingdom of God has already been spiritually inaugurated with the first coming of Christ, it will not be physically consummated until the second coming of Christ. Though the kingdom is currently spiritual, as Christ presently reigns in the hearts of those who believe, it will one day be physical at His second coming. Then, when Christ returns, the realm of Christ's dominion will extend from sea to sea, and the glory of the Lord will fill the earth (Hab. 2:14). But until then, "God's kingdom," as William Cox states, "exists as an incomplete realization awaiting its perfection at the appearing of the King of Glory."[22]

[22] Cox, *Biblical Studies in Final Things*, 43.

5

The Finality of
the Second Coming

My dad gave me some advice when I was younger that I will never forget and which impacted the way I have approached the Scriptures ever since. In fact, this advice anchored me in the amillennial position. My dad suggested I interpret the difficult passages of Scripture in light of the clear and direct passages of Scripture.

It was amazing to me that one of my theological professors turned this simple hermeneutical principle on its head. After arguing that we should take the symbolical and apocalyptical language of the book of Revelation literally, he went on to say that the language of 2 Peter 3 was to be understood symbolically. He said this, it seemed to me, because 2 Peter 3 contradicted his understanding of Revelation 20. Here he did the opposite of what my dad counseled me to do. My professor sought to interpret an easy-to-understand passage of Scripture, 2 Peter 3, in light of a very difficult passage, Revelation 20.

I couldn't accept his understanding of Revelation 20 because I was convinced that it was in opposition to the easy-to-understand passage of 2 Peter 3. When it comes to outlining end-time events, 2 Peter 3 is one of the clearest passages in Scripture. If I am to take the good counsel of my dad, then the more difficult passages of Scripture, such as Revelation 20, must be understood in light of the easier passages of Scripture and not the other way around. And when we read 2 Peter 3, we learn that the second coming of Christ brings about the end of the world. This also brings us to the fifth and last point of amillennialism—the *finality* of the second coming.

A Catastrophic Second Coming

According to the didactic passages of Scripture in the New Testament found in Matthew through Jude, there are certain events that will occur when Christ returns: (1) the general resurrection of the dead, (2) the destruction of the world, (3) the final judgment, and (4) the ushering in of the eternal state.

The General Resurrection

First, on that last day of human history, when Christ appears, the dead will rise again. The prophet Daniel spoke of a general resurrection: "And many of those who sleep in the dust of the earth shall awake, some to everlasting life, and some to shame and everlasting contempt" (Dan. 12:2). This general resurrection of the just and unjust was then confirmed by Christ: "An hour is coming when all who are in the tombs will hear his voice and come out, those who have done good to the resurrection of life, and those who have done evil to the resurrection of judgment" (John 5:28–29). This message was preached by Paul, who claimed that "there will be a resurrection of both the just and the unjust" (Acts 24:15).

Some in the church in Thessalonica were afraid of dying before the second coming of Christ because they were afraid of missing out on that glorious day of Christ's second coming. But, according to Paul, those who have died will not miss out. Those who are dead in Christ are already with the Lord, and when Christ returns, they, who are currently disembodied spirits, will return with Christ to meet their resurrected bodies. At His appearing, the dead will rise first and those who are alive will be caught up in the air and transformed with their new glorified bodies:

> But we do not want you to be uninformed, brothers, about those who are asleep, that you may not grieve as others do who have no hope. For since we believe that Jesus died and rose again, even so, through Jesus, God will bring with him those who have fallen asleep. For this we declare to you by a word from the Lord, that we who are alive, who are left until the coming of the Lord, will not precede those who have fallen asleep. For the Lord himself will descend from heaven with a cry of command, with the voice of an archangel, and with the sound of the trumpet of God. And the dead in Christ will rise first. Then we who are alive, who are left, will be caught up together with them in the clouds

> to meet the Lord in the air, and so we will always be with the Lord. Now concerning the times and the seasons, brothers, you have no need to have anything written to you. For you yourselves are fully aware that the day of the Lord will come like a thief in the night. While people are saying, "There is peace and security," then sudden destruction will come upon them as labor pains come upon a pregnant woman, and they will not escape. (1 Thess. 4:13—5:3)

Thus, we see that the day will come as a thief in the night when sudden destruction comes. This leads us to the second thing that will occur when the Lord returns.

The Destruction of the World

Christ warned of the destruction of the world at His return:

> For as in those days before the flood they were eating and drinking, marrying and giving in marriage, until the day when Noah entered the ark, and they were unaware until the flood came and swept them all away, so will be the coming of the Son of Man. Then two men will be in the field; one will be taken and one left. Two women will be grinding at the mill; one will be taken and one left. Therefore, stay awake, for you do not know on what day your Lord is coming. But know this, that if the master of the house had known in what part of the night the thief was coming, he would have stayed awake and would not have let his house be broken into. Therefore, you also must be ready, for the Son of

Man is coming at an hour you do not expect. (Matt. 24:38–44)

And this warning was reaffirmed by Peter when he said,

> But the day of the Lord will come like a thief, and then the heavens will pass away with a roar, and the heavenly bodies will be burned up and dissolved, and the earth and the works that are done on it will be exposed. Since all these things are thus to be dissolved, what sort of people ought you to be in lives of holiness and godliness, waiting for and hastening the coming of the day of God, because of which the heavens will be set on fire and dissolved, and the heavenly bodies will melt as they burn! But according to his promise we are waiting for new heavens and a new earth in which righteousness dwells. Therefore, beloved, since you are waiting for these, be diligent to be found by him without spot or blemish, and at peace. (2 Peter 3:10–14)

The Day of Judgment

The last day will be a day of final judgment. According to the parable of the wheat and the tares, both the true believers and false believers will remain together until the harvest at the end of the age. Then Christ will come, sending His holy angels to separate the tares from the wheat, "gather[ing] out of his kingdom all causes of sin and all law-breakers." The tares will be bound in bundles to be burned and thrown "into the fiery furnace. In that place there will be weeping and gnashing of teeth" (Matt. 13:41–42). But the wheat will be gathered into the barn as "the righteous will shine like the sun in the kingdom of their Father" (v. 43).

All the dead will rise when Christ comes to judge the world (Acts 17:31). He warned, "Behold, I am coming soon, bringing my recompense with me, to repay everyone for what he has done" (Rev. 22:12). For Christ declared,

> When the Son of Man comes in his glory, and all the angels with him, then he will sit on his glorious throne. Before him will be gathered all the nations, and he will separate people one from another as a shepherd separates the sheep from the goats. And he will place the sheep on his right, but the goats on the left. Then the King will say to those on his right, "Come, you who are blessed by my Father, inherit the kingdom prepared for you from the foundation of the world. For I was hungry and you gave me food, I was thirsty and you gave me drink, I was a stranger and you welcomed me." (Matt. 25:31)

Paul speaks of the day of judgment as the day that the saints will be eternally glorified and the wicked will be eternally condemned:

> This is evidence of the righteous judgment of God, that you may be considered worthy of the kingdom of God, for which you are also suffering—since indeed God considers it just to repay with affliction those who

afflict you, and to grant relief to you who are afflicted as well as to us, when the Lord Jesus is revealed from heaven with his mighty angels in flaming fire, inflicting vengeance on those who do not know God and on those who do not obey the gospel of our Lord Jesus. They will suffer the punishment of eternal destruction, away from the presence of the Lord and from the glory of his might, when he comes on that day to be glorified in his saints, and to be marveled at among all who have believed, because our testimony to you was believed. (2 Thess. 1:5–10)

It will be at this time that Christ brings every nation into subjection to His lordship: "'Therefore wait for me,' declares the LORD, 'for the day when I rise up to seize the prey. For my decision is to gather nations, to assemble kingdoms, to pour out upon them my indignation, all my burning anger; for in the fire of my jealousy all the earth shall be consumed'" (Zeph. 3:8). Though He had no interest in going to war with the nations at His first coming, at His second coming Christ will come to conquer the kingdoms of this world: "From his mouth comes a sharp sword with which to strike down the nations, and he will rule them with a rod of iron. He will tread the winepress of the fury of the wrath of God the Almighty. On his robe and on his thigh he has a name written, King of kings and Lord of lords" (Rev. 19:15–16).

When Christ returns, no one will escape. There will be nowhere to hide. This is why Peter urges everyone to make sure that they are right with God now. *Today* is the day of salvation. Once the sky splits open and the clouds roll back like a scroll, it will be too late. We must be prepared now, for Christ is coming as a thief in the night. We are to watch and be ready, as the Lord warned us, for we do not know the day or the hour (Matt. 25:12). Once He appears, there is no longer hope of salvation. There is no salvation on this day or any day afterward for, as we see in the next point, the last day is the first day of eternity.

The Eternal State

The kingdom of God that was inaugurated at Jesus Christ's first coming will be consummated at His second coming. Christ is not starting to build His kingdom, as some suggest, but is about to hand over a completed and perfected kingdom to the Father. In other words, when Christ presents a perfect kingdom to God the Father, this marks the end of the world:

> Then comes the end, when he delivers the kingdom to God the Father after destroying every rule and every authority and power. For he must reign until he has put all his enemies under his feet. The last enemy to be destroyed is death. For "God has put all things in subjection under his feet." But when it says, "all things are put in subjection," it is plain that he is excepted who put all things in subjection under him. When all things are subjected to him, then the Son himself will also be subjected to him who put all things in subjection under him, that God may be all in all. (1 Cor. 15:24–28)

After the world is destroyed by fire, God will create a new heaven and a new earth where only the righteous dwell with God forever. At that time, "He will swallow up death forever; and the Lord GOD will wipe away tears from all faces, and the reproach of his people he will take away from all the earth, for the LORD has spoken" (Isa. 25:8). Then the promise to David will finally be realized in full. The son of David will have built David a house where the people of God will dwell with Him in the promised land in peace forever:

> Then I saw a new heaven and a new earth, for the first heaven and the first earth had passed away, and the sea was no more. And I saw the holy city, new Jerusalem, coming down out of heaven from God, prepared as a bride adorned for her husband. And I heard a loud voice from the throne saying, "Behold, the dwelling place of God is with man. He will dwell with them, and they will be his people, and God himself will be with them as their God. He will wipe away every tear from their eyes, and death shall be no more, neither shall there be mourning, nor crying, nor pain anymore, for the former things have passed away." (Rev. 21:1–4)

No Literal One-Thousand-Year Reign

If we are to use all these didactic and clear passages of Scripture to understand the difficult passages of Scripture, then Revelation 20 cannot be speaking of a literal thousand years where the righteous and the unrighteous live together in peace under the rule of Christ. It is not possible because there is no room for a thousand-year period after the second coming of Christ. The Bible makes it clear that the world ends at the very moment Christ returns. Once Christ comes again, there is (1) no more hope for salvation, (2) no more time for the wicked to live on the earth, and (3) no more time for the wicked to live alongside the righteous.

And this is what the theological term *amillennial* means—"no (literal) millennial." The *a* is a negative prefix, and the word *millennial* is taken from Revelation 20 where John speaks of Satan being bound for a thousand years (i.e., a millennium). Therefore, amillennialists believe that the reign of Christ alluded to in Revelation 20:1–3 refers to the spiritual reign of Christ that extends between the first and second coming of Christ, not to a future thousand-year period that takes place after the second coming of Christ.

Revelation 20:1–3

We must remember that it's not Peter or Paul but John who utilized symbolic and apocalyptical language. In fact, in the very first sentence of the book of Revelation, John tells us that the visions contained in his letter had been shown to him through signs and symbols: "The Revelation of Jesus Christ, which God gave Him to show His servants—things which must shortly take place. And He sent and *signified it* by His angel to His servant John" (Rev. 1:1 NKJV). The word translated here as "signified" is the Greek word *sémainó*, which means "to signify" or "to give a sign." It comes from the root word *séma*, which means "a sign" or "a mark."

Though the visions in the book of Revelation are not the same as the parables of Christ, they are similar in that they communicate truth through a parabolic story. The parable of the sower, for instance, must be interpreted figuratively. Preaching the gospel can be compared to sowing seeds, but those preaching the gospel are not actually sowing literal seeds. In the parable of the sower, seeds represent the gospel. The different types of soils also, according to Christ, represent different types of hearers of the gospel (Matt. 13:1–23).

In the same way, the signs and visions and apocalyptic language of the book of Revelation are not to be taken literally. I don't know of anyone who doesn't acknowledge that at least some of the language in Revelation is symbolic. As just a few examples, John saw (1) seven stars, which represented the seven angels of seven churches, (2) seven golden lampstands, which represented the seven churches of Asia, (3) a sword coming out of the mouth of Christ, which represented the divine judgment that comes from the mouth of Christ, and (4) a red dragon, which represented Satan. The list of symbols goes on.

Just as preaching the gospel is compared to sowing seeds, the seven as of the seven churches are compared to seven stars in Revelation. Hopefully, however, no one thinks these angels are literal stars. We should be careful not to interpret symbols as literal realties, such as literal stars, literal lampstands, a literal red dragon, and a literal sword protruding out of the mouth of Christ.

And if we can agree that the visions of Revelation are full of symbolic language, should we not also agree that such symbolism is more challenging to interpret than the literal and didactic language of Paul and Peter? Surely, we can agree that the more difficult passages of Scripture will not disagree with the more direct and clearer passages of Scripture.

With the symbolic language of Revelation and the literal language of 2 Peter 3 in mind, should we not come to the conclusion that the thousand years spoken of in Revelation 20:1–3 is not actually referring to a literal thousand years? If 2 Peter 3 does not allow for a thousand-year time period to exist between the second coming and the destruction of the world, then we must conclude that the thousand years in Revelation 20 is speaking of a symbolic (perfect or complete) period of time.

This understanding is reinforced by the fact that Revelation 20 is full of symbolic language. That particular vision includes a chain, a seal, a bottomless pit, and a red dragon:

> Then I saw an angel coming down from heaven, holding in his hand the key to the bottomless pit and a great chain. And he seized the dragon, that ancient serpent, who is the devil and Satan, and bound him for a thousand years, and threw him into the pit, and shut it and sealed it over him, so that he might not deceive

the nations any longer, until the thousand years were ended. After that he must be released for a little while. (Rev. 20:1–3)

It would be hard to imagine that a physical chain and a physical seal would be able to bind Satan and that a physical bottomless pit can hold Satan—a spiritual being. It's even harder to imagine that this bottomless pit has a literal key that opens and closes it. And we know for a fact that Satan is not a literal red dragon. In fact, John makes sure we understand that the red dragon represents the devil.

No doubt John saw a red dragon being bound by an angel. John saw, as if the vision were acted out before him in a cosmic play in the heavens, an angel coming from heaven with a key in his hand to open the pit into which the red dragon, bound by a chain, would be thrown. And the same angel that bound the dragon ends up releasing the dragon.

But, like Nebuchadnezzar's dream or the parables of Christ, this vision must be deciphered. The symbols must be interpreted. And surely, like Nebuchadnezzar's dream and the parables of Christ, the symbols in this vision are not meant to be taken literally.

Are we to believe that the key, chain, dragon, seal, and bottomless pit are all symbols that represent spiritual realities, but the thousand years are to be taken literally? Other numbers in the book of Revelation, such as the numbers 7 and 666, are symbolic. The number 7 represents perfection, and 666 represents man (see Rev. 13:18). Could the number 1,000 also be symbolic and represent a spiritual reality?

When it is said that God owns all "the cattle on a thousand hills" (Ps. 50:10), are we to think that God only owns the cattle on a thousand hills? Is that to be taken literally? Does it not make more sense to think the phrase "a thousand hills" is parabolic language representing all the cattle in the world?

The thousand-year period in Revelation 20 is also a parabolic way of saying a perfect or complete amount of time. In other words, Satan will be bound for the full amount of time needed—not one day sooner or one day later. For the full amount of time, the devil will be bound. Christ will be able to do all His work without being prevented by Satan.

Thus, it makes more sense to view the millennial reign of Christ in Revelation 20 as symbolizing the spiritual reign of Christ that is currently taking place between His first and second comings, for Paul says that Christ must reign until He puts all His enemies under His feet. "Then comes the end," Paul says, "when he delivers the kingdom to God the Father after destroying every rule and every authority and power" (1 Cor. 15:24).

With 2 Peter 3 and 1 Corinthians 15 in mind, it seems apparent that Revelation 20 cannot be teaching a future thousand-year reign of Christ on the earth (that is to take place after the second coming and that consists of believers and unbelievers). It seems more possible that the thousand years is merely symbolic of an undisclosed but perfect time period between the first and second coming of Christ.

But the obvious objection is that the red dragon is supposed to be bound during this time, and we all know that Satan is currently walking about like a lion seeking someone to devour (1 Peter 5:8).

If we read closely, however, we see an important detail about the nature and extent of the binding of Satan. Just as John gives us the meaning of the red dragon, he gives us the meaning of the binding: "so that he might not deceive the nations any longer" (Rev. 20:3). In other words, we learn that Satan is restricted in such a way that he is no longer able to hold the nations of the world captive to his lies and deception. This is the point of this passage. Floyd Hamilton explains it this way:

> I suppose that no one would insist that Satan is to be bound with a literal chain of iron or some other metal, for Satan is a spirit and material chains could not hold him captive for a moment. Binding always means the limitation of power in some way. When men bound themselves with an oath not to do something, they agreed to limit their own power and rights to the extent of their oaths. A man and wife are bound by their marriage vows, but that does not mean that they are bound in respect to other relationships in life. . . . So Satan's being bound does not mean that he is powerless to tempt people, and we know that he does. It is merely

limitation of Satan's power in one particular respect especially, that of ability to "deceive the nations." During the interadventual period the gospel is to be proclaimed to all nations, and Satan is powerless to prevent it. The way of salvation has been opened to all nations and there is nothing that Satan can do to block that way.[23]

We must ask ourselves: When was Satan dethroned? When was the Prince of Darkness cast out? When was the great deceiver's head crushed? When did his grip of deception on the nations begin to slip? When was the devil defeated?

The answer is that Satan was defeated by Christ at the cross! It was at the cross that Satan lost his legal authority over the nations. The Son of God came in the weakness of the flesh of Adam and Eve "that through death he might destroy the one who has the power of death, that is, the devil, and deliver all those who through fear of death were subject to lifelong slavery" (Heb. 2:14–15). At the cross is when Satan, the strong man, was bound by an even stronger man (Matt. 12:29).

Though Satan is still roaming around like a lion, seeking to devour whomever he can (knowing now that his time is short), he has been mortally wounded. His power has been stripped from him, even bound, if you would. For the first time since the fall, Satan's power has been legally taken

from him and given to the seed of the woman—Christ
Jesus. The legal rights that Satan had over the nations of
the world have been transferred to the son of David.

All power in heaven and earth has been given to a
man—the seed of the woman and the son of David:

> Then I saw in the right hand of him who was seated on
> the throne a scroll written within and on the back, sealed
> with seven seals. And I saw a mighty angel proclaiming
> with a loud voice, "Who is worthy to open the scroll and
> break its seals?" And no one in heaven or on earth or
> under the earth was able to open the scroll or to look into
> it, and I began to weep loudly because no one was found
> worthy to open the scroll or to look into it. And one of the
> elders said to me, "Weep no more; behold, the Lion of the
> tribe of Judah, the Root of David, has conquered, so that
> he can open the scroll and its seven seals." . . .
>
> And they sang a new song, saying,
>
> "Worthy are you to take the scroll
>   and to open its seals,
> for you were slain, and by your blood you ransomed
> people for God
>   from every tribe and language and people and nation,
> and you have made them a kingdom and priests to our
> God,
>   and they shall reign on the earth."
>
> Then I looked, and I heard around the throne and the
> living creatures and the elders the voice of many angels,

numbering myriads of myriads and thousands of thousands, saying with a loud voice,

"Worthy is the Lamb who was slain,
to receive power and wealth and wisdom and might
and honor and glory and blessing!"

And I heard every creature in heaven and on earth and under the earth and in the sea, and all that is in them, saying,

"To him who sits on the throne and to the Lamb
be blessing and honor and glory and might forever and
ever!"

And the four living creatures said, "Amen!" and the elders fell down and worshiped. (Revelation 5)

The seed of the woman, the root of David, stands victorious. Like David standing over the dead body of Goliath with his head held high in his hand, Christ stands over the defeated Serpent. "He," at the cross, "disarmed the rulers and authorities and put them to open shame, by triumphing over them in him" (Col. 2:15).

With His victory over the kingdom of darkness, Christ's first order of business was to commission the gospel to go into all the world. With the walls of deception broken, Christ commissions the church to go and rescue the perishing from the grip of the great deceiver (Matthew 28). Go and preach the gospel to every soul. Now that the prince of the power of the air has been cast out, and now that all power in heaven and earth has been given to the Son of Man, no territory is off limits and no people group is unreachable. The gates of hell have been shattered and can no longer keep the gospel from coming in and plundering the kingdom of darkness of its prisoners.

This great defeat is depicted in John's vision as a red dragon being chained and bound for a thousand years. This does not mean Satan no longer deceives, for the Bible says, "If our gospel is veiled, it is veiled to those who are perishing. In their case the god of this world has blinded the minds of the unbelievers, to keep them from seeing the light of the gospel of the glory of Christ, who is the image of God" (2 Cor. 4:3–4). It does mean that Satan can no longer keep the gospel from going into all the world and rescuing the spiritual children of Abraham out of every nation, tribe, and people group of the world. As my father, Donald Johnson, states in his commentary on Revelation:

> Therefore, in this chapter we see the glorious truth that Satan is limited and restrained and cast out regarding his diabolical plan to keep the nations in utter ignorance and deception until Christ and the gospel have completed their mission with mankind.[24]

Now that the strong man has been bound and the kingdom of God has come, the gates of hell can no longer keep the good news from going to every nation and people

---

[24] Donald R. Johnson, *Victory in Jesus: A Devotional Commentary on the Book of Revelation* (Conway, AR: Free Grace Press, 2018), 290.

group of the world (Matt. 16:18). For both Jews and gentiles, the gospel is the power of God unto salvation (Rom. 1:16).

And not only did Christ commission us to go, He promised He would go with us. Until the end of the age, Christ will travel to the ends of the earth through His messengers to call out His people to Himself (Matt. 28:20). That is, Christ, through the Spirit and the church, will continue to build His kingdom, one conversion at a time, until He has gathered all Abraham's promised children from out of every nation and people group.

Then, at the end of the age, the dragon is released from the bottomless pit, as Revelation 20 reveals, which indicates that the nations will once again be deceived by Satan. And if this is the case, it corresponds with the dire prophecy of Christ Jesus when He said, "When the Son of Man comes, will he find faith on earth?" (Luke 18:8). The implication of this rhetorical question is that true faith will be scarce.

When I think of this vision in Revelation 20, I almost always think of the times I have watched a bag of popcorn being cooked in a microwave. At first, no kernels are popping. Things start off slow. Like watching water boil, it seems to take forever. Those first pops are like the few conversions we read about in the Old Testament: Abraham, Moses, David, and Jeremiah, and though at one point God had reserved seven thousand people for Himself, that is really not a lot of people in relation to the world's population at that time—it was just a small remnant within a relatively small nation among all the nations of the world.

But suddenly there is an explosion of popping. And this is like when the Spirit was poured out on the day of Pentecost. First there were three thousand conversions and then another five thousand a few days later (Acts 2:41; 4:4). Things sped up abruptly. Christianity spread fast. Something changed. Swiftly the gospel traveled from Jerusalem, with a handful of Jewish disciples, into Judea and then into all the world. People of all types of ethnicities were flooding into the kingdom of God. Before the end of the first century, churches were planted everywhere across the known world. Truly, in the seed of Abraham, all the nations of the world have been blessed. And this explosion of Jewish and gentile conversions corresponds with the binding of Satan.

But at the very end of the cooking process, again only a few kernels here and there are popping. And so it seems that at the end of the age there will be just a few remaining elect to be gathered into the bosom of Abraham. It is as if God unleashes the dragon to prepare and ripen the world for judgment (Rev. 14:14–20).

It says that the dragon *must* be released (Rev. 20:3), which implies Christ has a purpose for the deceiver. It is as if Christ binds Satan and freely goes into a new territory to gather His people out of Satan's grip, and once He has rescued those for whom He came into the world, He unleashes Satan on those who rejected Him. As it is written, "The coming of the lawless one is by the activity of Satan with all power and false signs and wonders, and with all wicked deception for those who are perishing, because they refused to love the truth and so be saved. Therefore God sends them a strong delusion, so that they may believe what is false, in order that all may be condemned who did not believe the truth but had pleasure in unrighteousness" (2 Thess. 2:9–12). This is a scary concept for those who think they can turn to Christ whenever they wish. Christ may just turn Satan loose upon them.

In the end, amillennialism does not reject the reign of Christ; it simply denies that the reign of Christ is restricted to a literal thousand-year period. Cornelis Venema summarizes amillennialism this way:

> Amillennialism regards the millennium of Revelation 20 to be a symbolical representation of the present reign of Christ with his saints. During the period of time between Christ's first advent and his return at the end of the age, Satan has been bound in order to no longer deceive the nations. The millennium is not a literal period of one thousand years but represents the complete period during which God has granted Christ the authority to receive the nations as his inheritance.[25]

---

[25] Cornelis Venema, *Christ and the Future: The Bible's Teaching About the Last Things* (Edinburgh: Banner of Truth, 2008), 108.

Conclusion

Regardless of whether we can make sense of Revelation 20:1–3, the events sounding the second coming of Christ, as revealed to us in the didactic passages of the New Testament, rule out the possibility of a literal thousand-year reign of Christ. We learn in those passages of Scripture that the second coming of Christ will be the end of the world. The world will be destroyed, the wicked will be judged, and the righteous will inherit the new earth.

Until then, let us prepare ourselves for the Lord's coming by making sure we have submitted ourselves to His lordship before it's too late. Let us bow the knee to His reign now while there is still hope of salvation. For Christ is on the throne, and He must continue to reign until He has subdued all His enemies under His footstool.

In summary, the redemptive-historical hermeneutic, which is the first point of amillennialism, leads us to the second point of amillennialism—that the intended children of Abraham are those, and only those, who are united to Christ by faith. Those who are Abraham's children by faith are the true heirs of Abraham.

The third point of amillennialism is that the kingdom of God is currently spiritual. Since His first coming Christ has been seated on the throne of David and will continue to rule and reign from heaven until He finishes building the kingdom with the redeemed and delivers it, without spot or blemish, to God the Father on the last day.

The fourth point of amillennialism is that the promised land is the new earth. Abraham was not looking for a piece of land that remained under the curse of the fall; he was looking for a city whose builder and maker was God. It will not be until the new creation that the resurrected Abraham, with all his glorified children, will dwell forever with God on the earth in perfect peace.

The fifth point of amillennialism is the finality of the second coming of Christ. The only hope of salvation is now—before the second coming of Christ. He will come like a thief in the night, but once He appears, the just and the unjust will rise from the dead, the world will be destroyed with fire, and everyone will face God in judgment to either be cast into the lake of fire or to enter into God's eternal rest.

Amillennialism is not complex. It's simply the gospel applied to the history of the world.